Pixel
PUZZLES

Publications International, Ltd.

ADD SOME COLOR TO YOUR LIFE

Remember how much fun coloring books were when you were a little kid? With the puzzles in this book, you can experience that fun again, and add in a whole new layer of challenge. Each black-and-white image comes with a color key. Using the color key as a guide, you'll color in the image. As you do, you'll reveal a hidden picture.

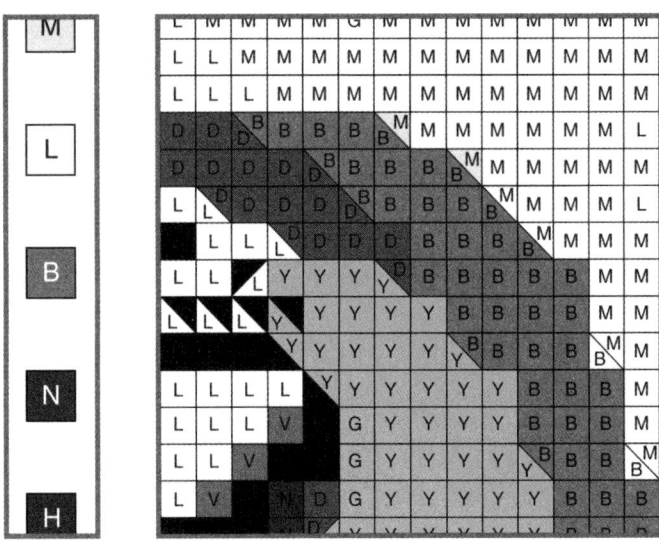

You'll discover penguins and parachutes, lighthouses and sunflowers. We've even included a few do-it-yourself optical illusions! At the back of the book, you'll find a full-color answer key showing the filled-in picture, as well as the original photograph or illustration that was used to create the picture.

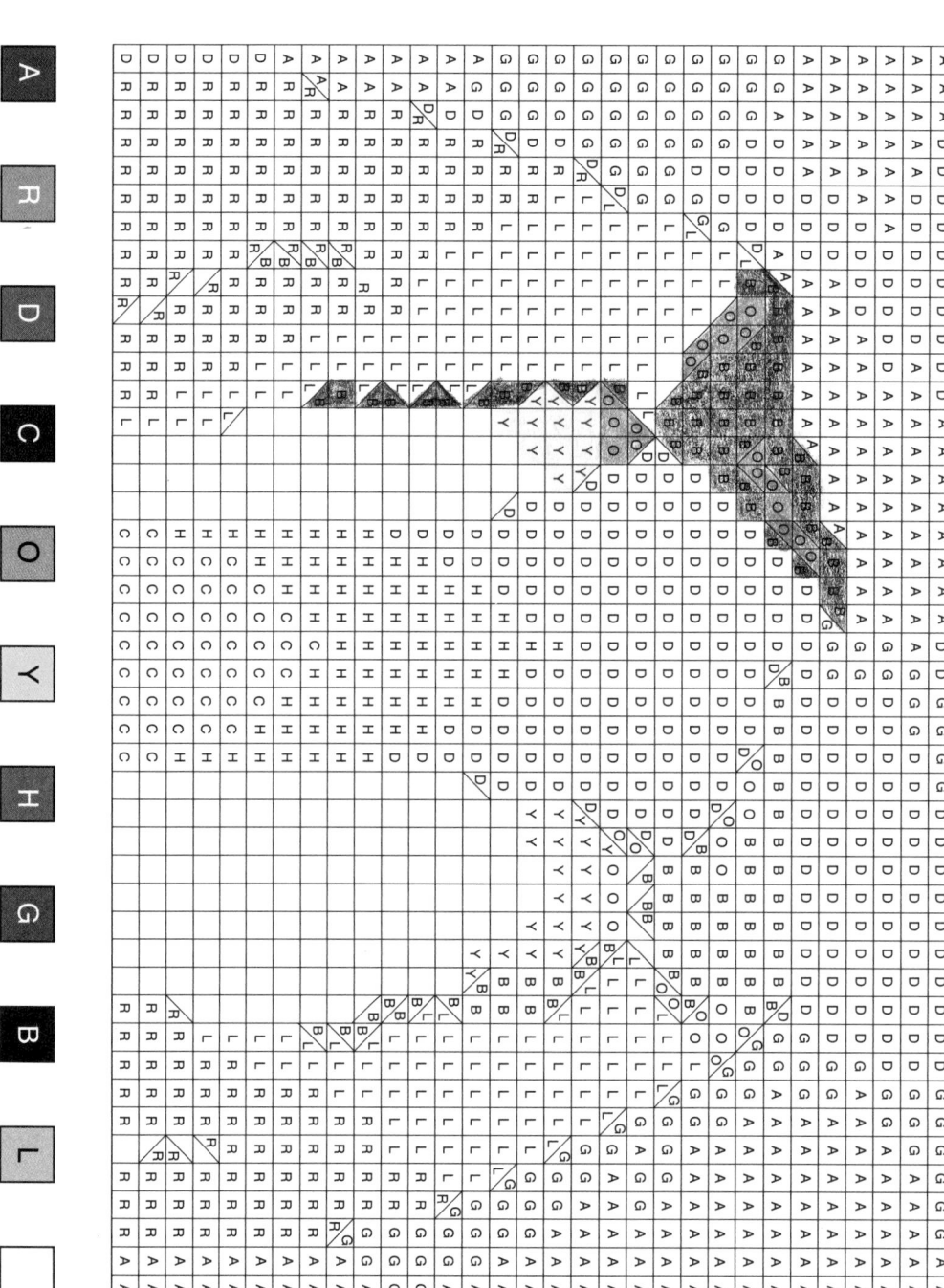

PIECE IT TOGETHER

A GUSTY GATHERING

SUN SEEKER

A
B
C
D
E
G
H
I
J
K
L
M
N
O
Q
R
S
U
W
Y
Z

Answer on page 107.

OUT OF THE SAND

WHAT GOES UP...

Answer on page 108.

LOUNGE LOVER?

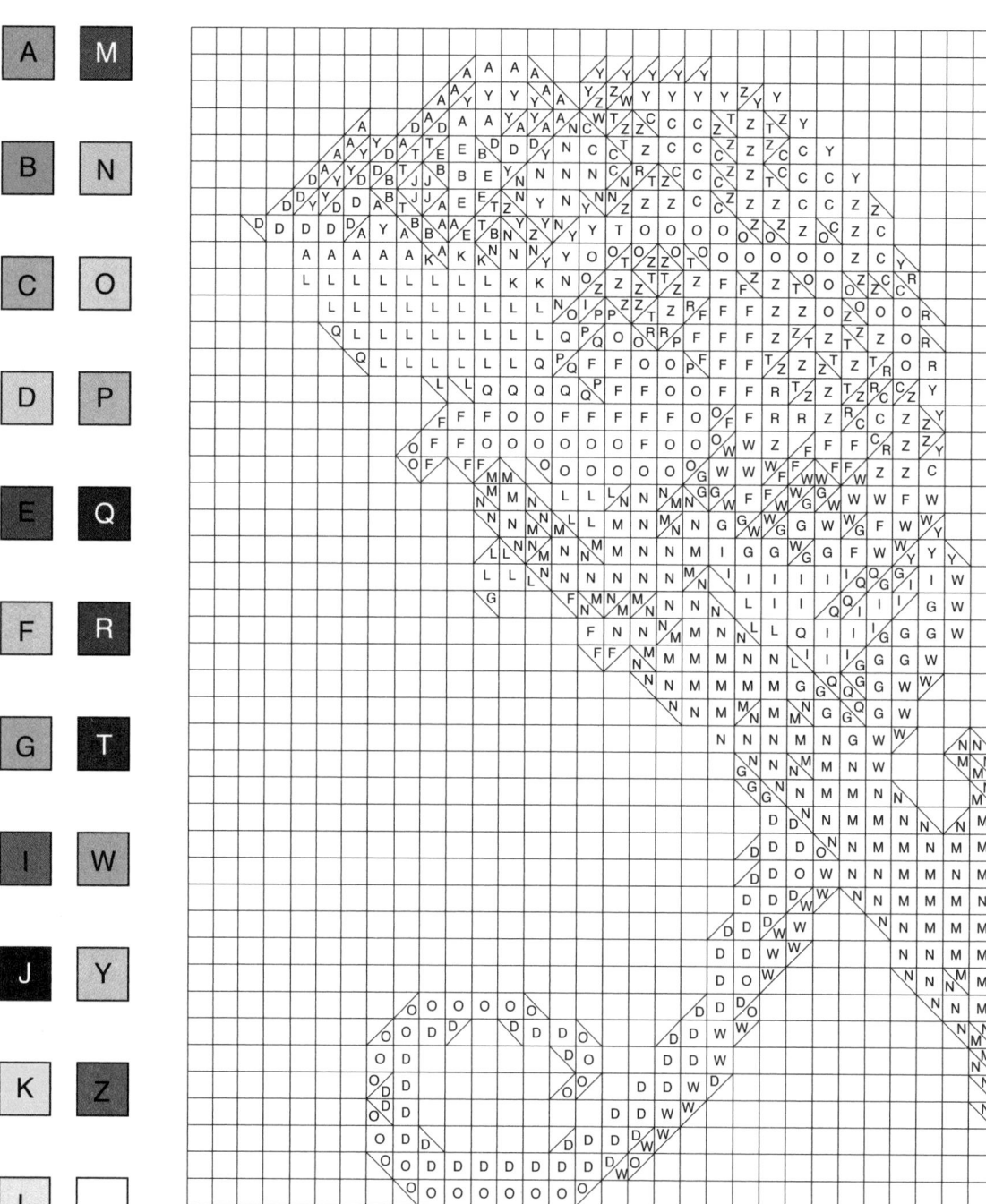

A B C D E F G H I J K L M N O P Q R S T

11

Answer on page 109.

HOP TO IT

Answer on page 110.

TICKLED PINK

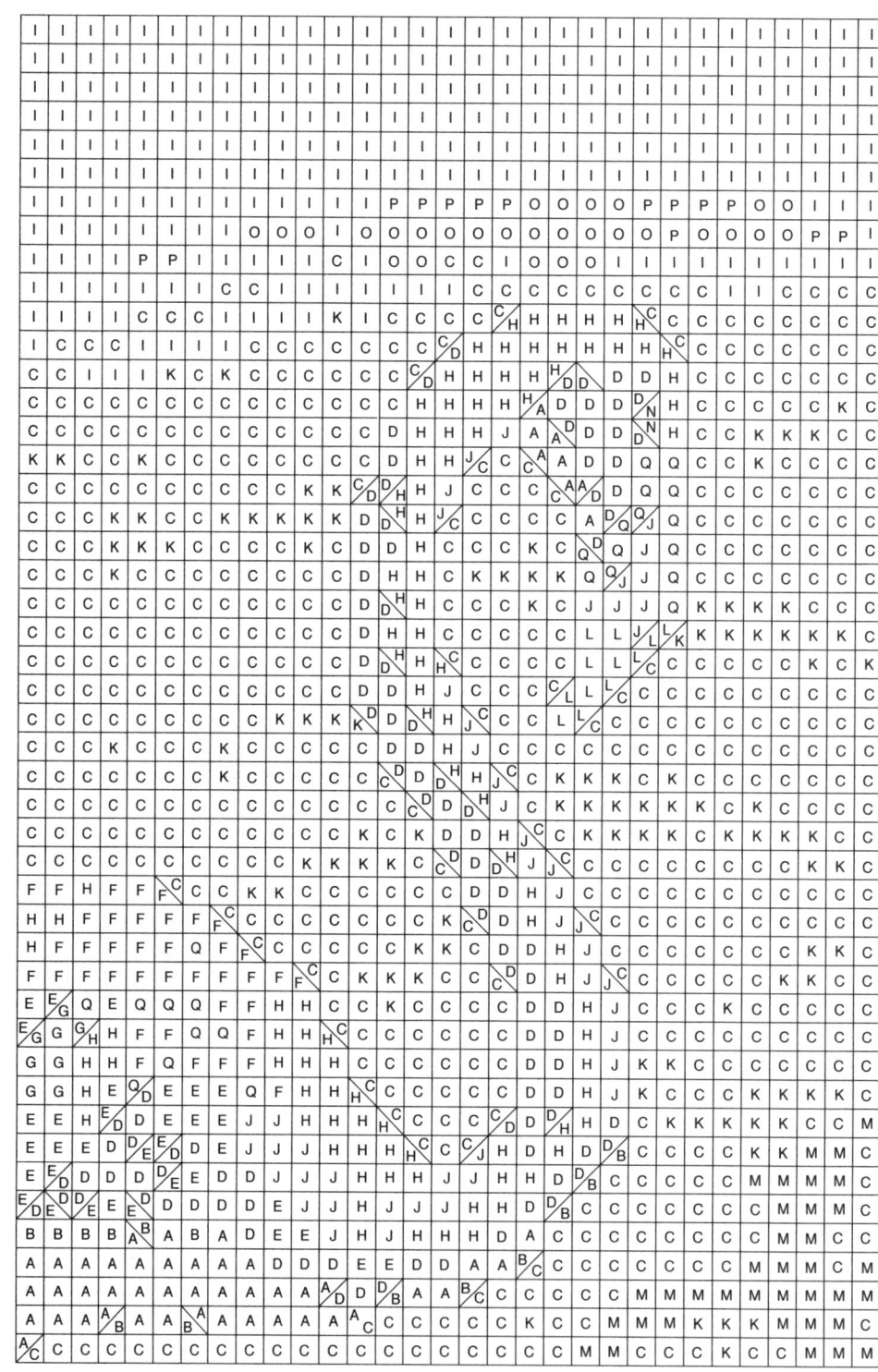

A UNIQUE ARRANGEMENT

15

Answer on page 111.

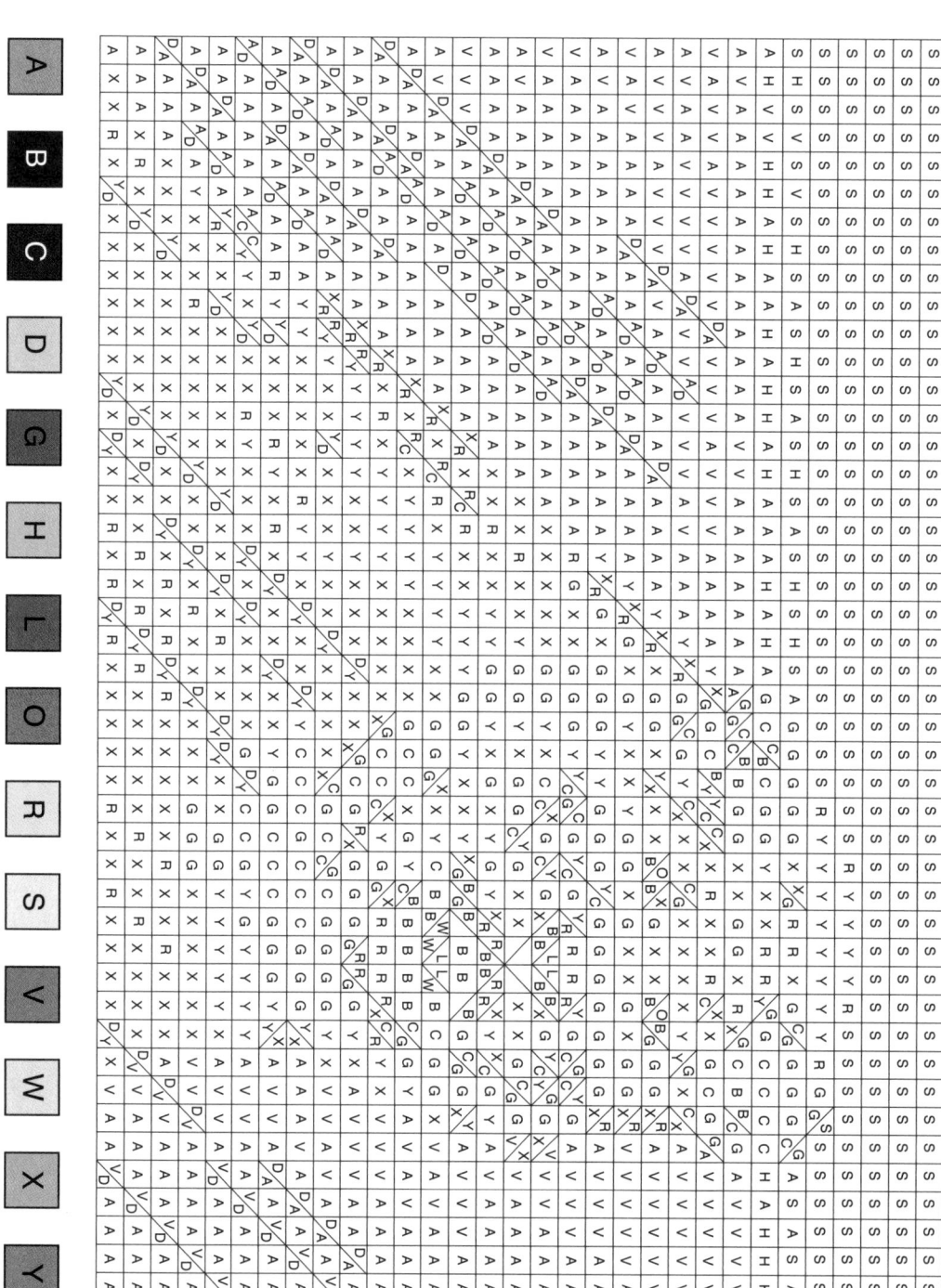

Answer on page 112.

WHEN IT POURS

Answer on page 112.

OUT OF THIS WORLD

 A
 B
 C
 D
 E
 F
 G
 H
 I
 J

 K
L M N O P Q R S

Answer on page 113.

A TALL ORDER

Answer on page 113.

ALL AFLUTTER

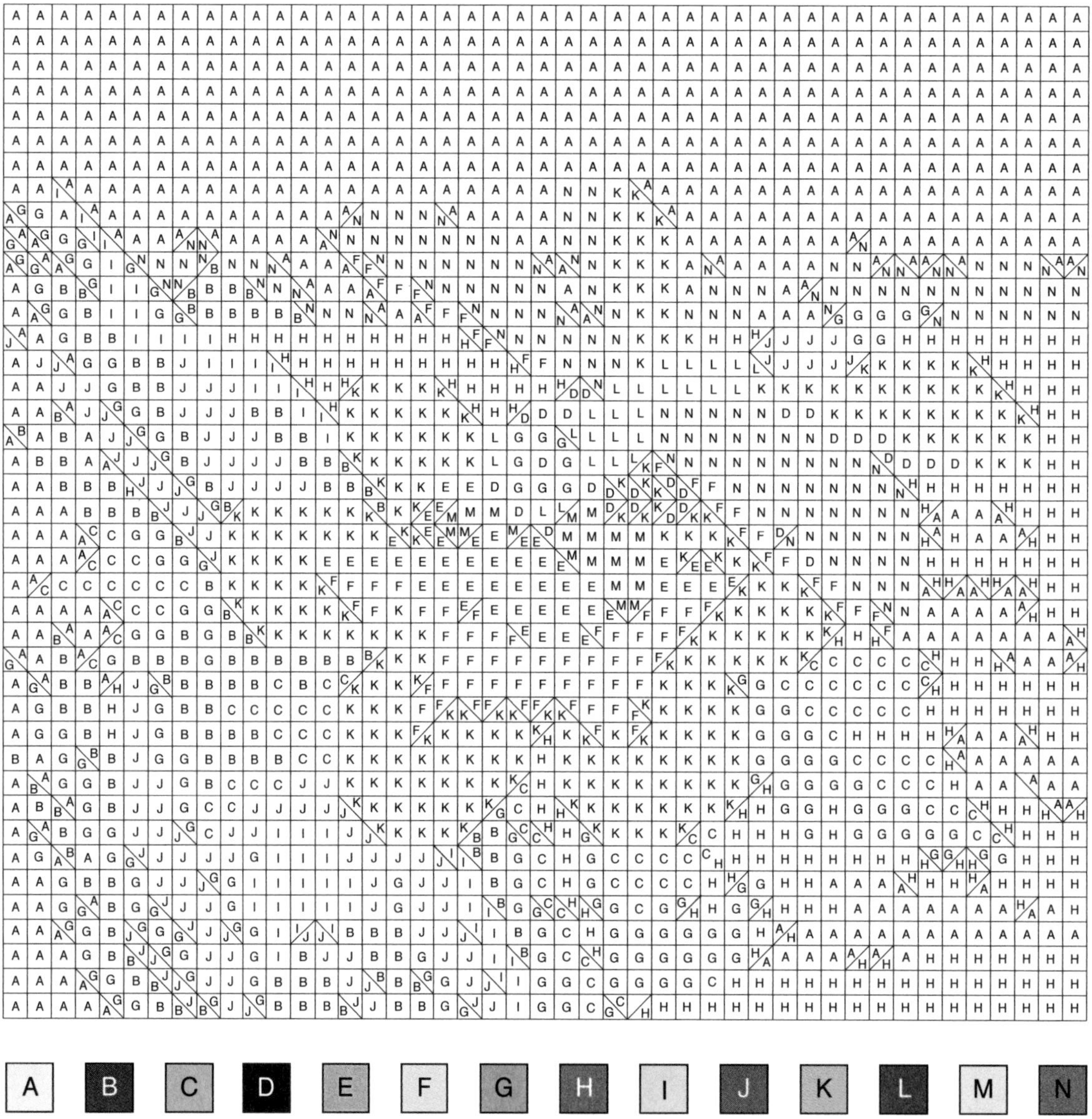

Answer on page 114.

BEAM ME UP

21

MANE EVENT

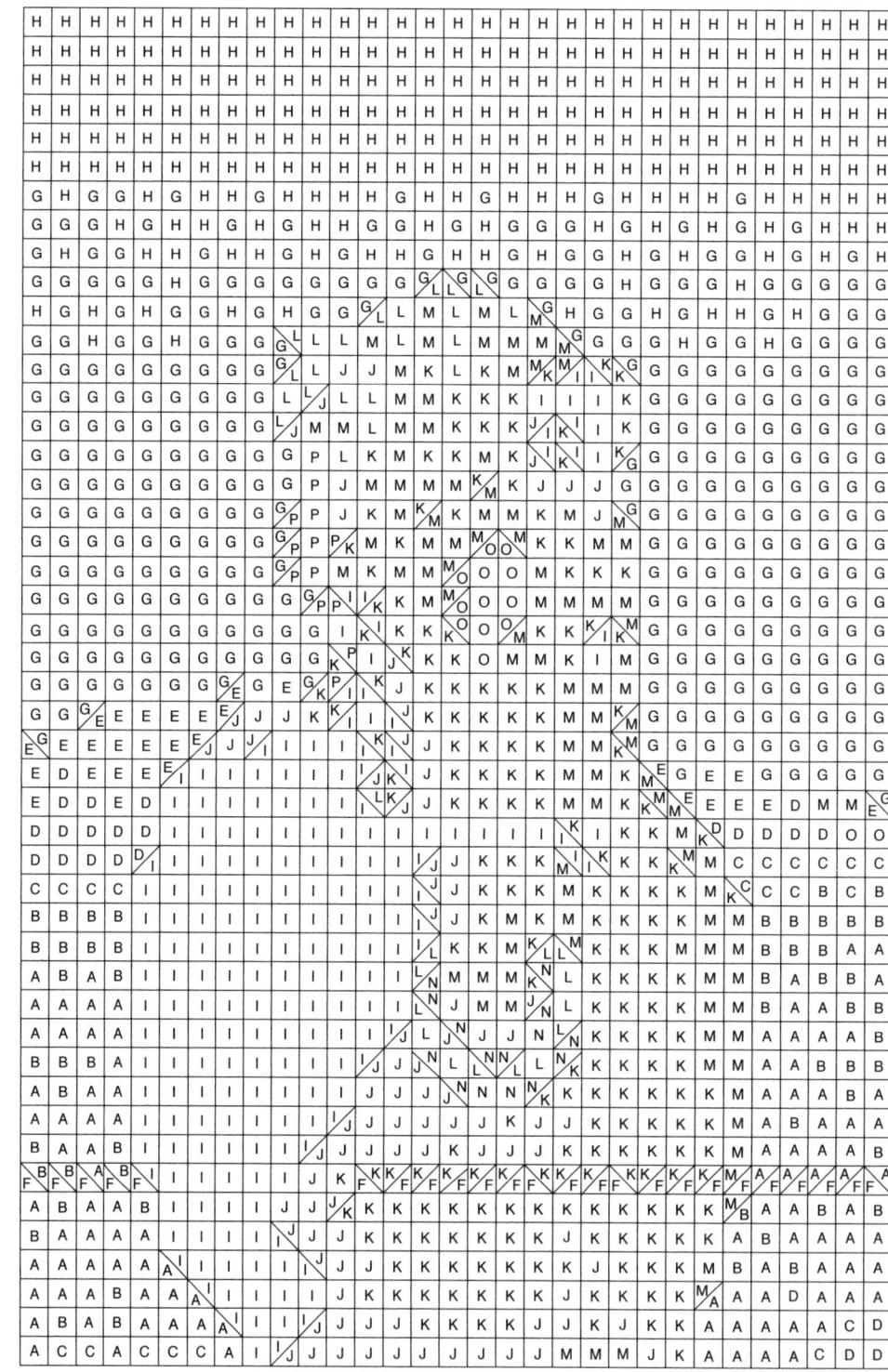

Answer on page 115.

UP IN THE AIR

Answer on page 115.

TRUNK SHOW

NEED FOR SPEED

Answer on page 116.

HE LOVES ME (OR NOT)

A B C D E F G H I J K L M N O

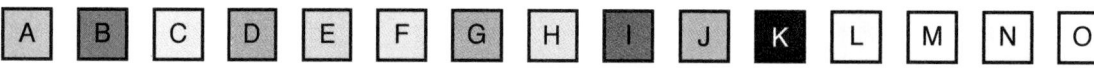

Answer on page 117.

Answer on page 117.

Answer on page 118.

ONE WAY TO GET AROUND

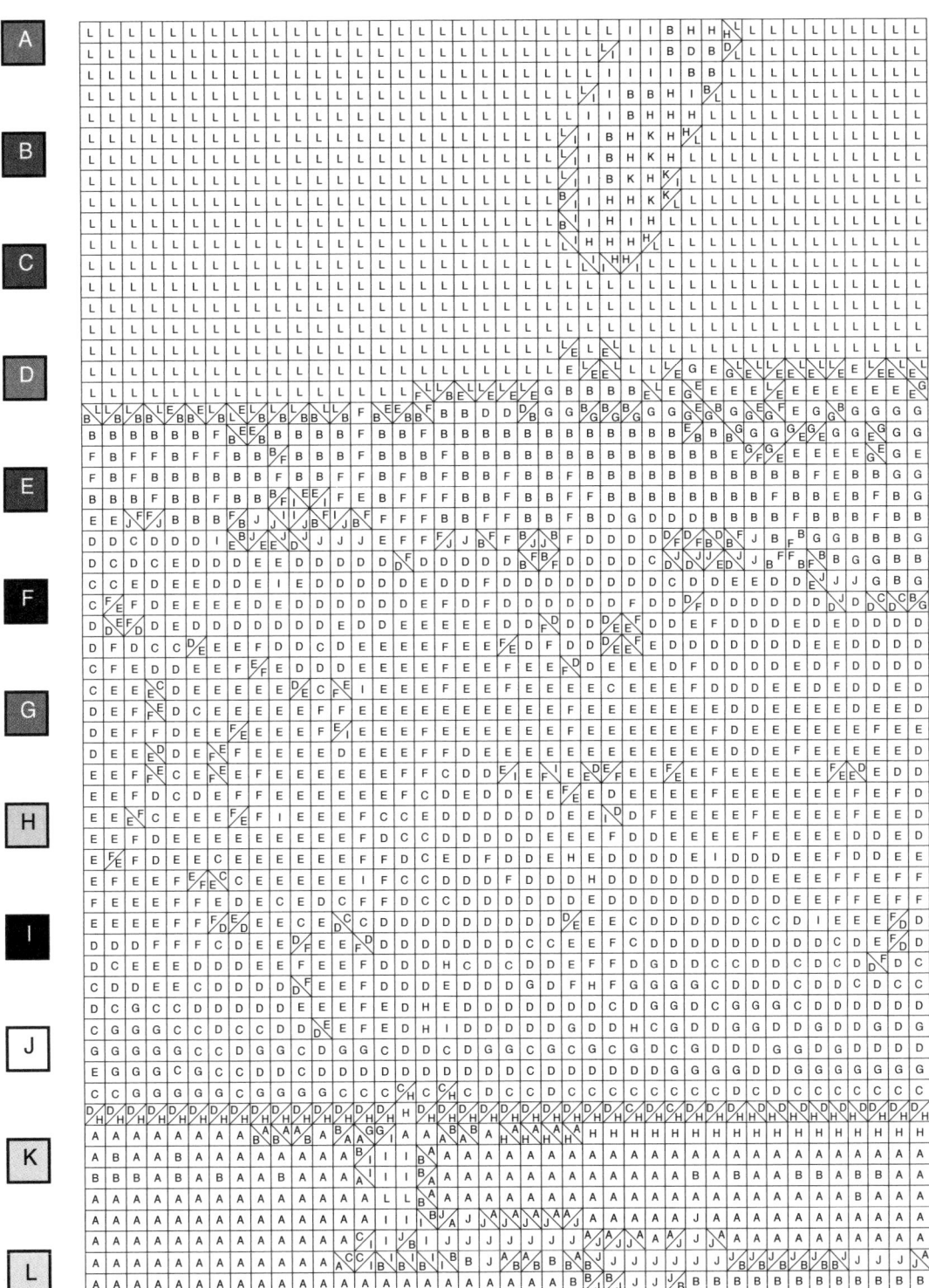

Answer on page 118.

NECTAR AND AMBROSIA

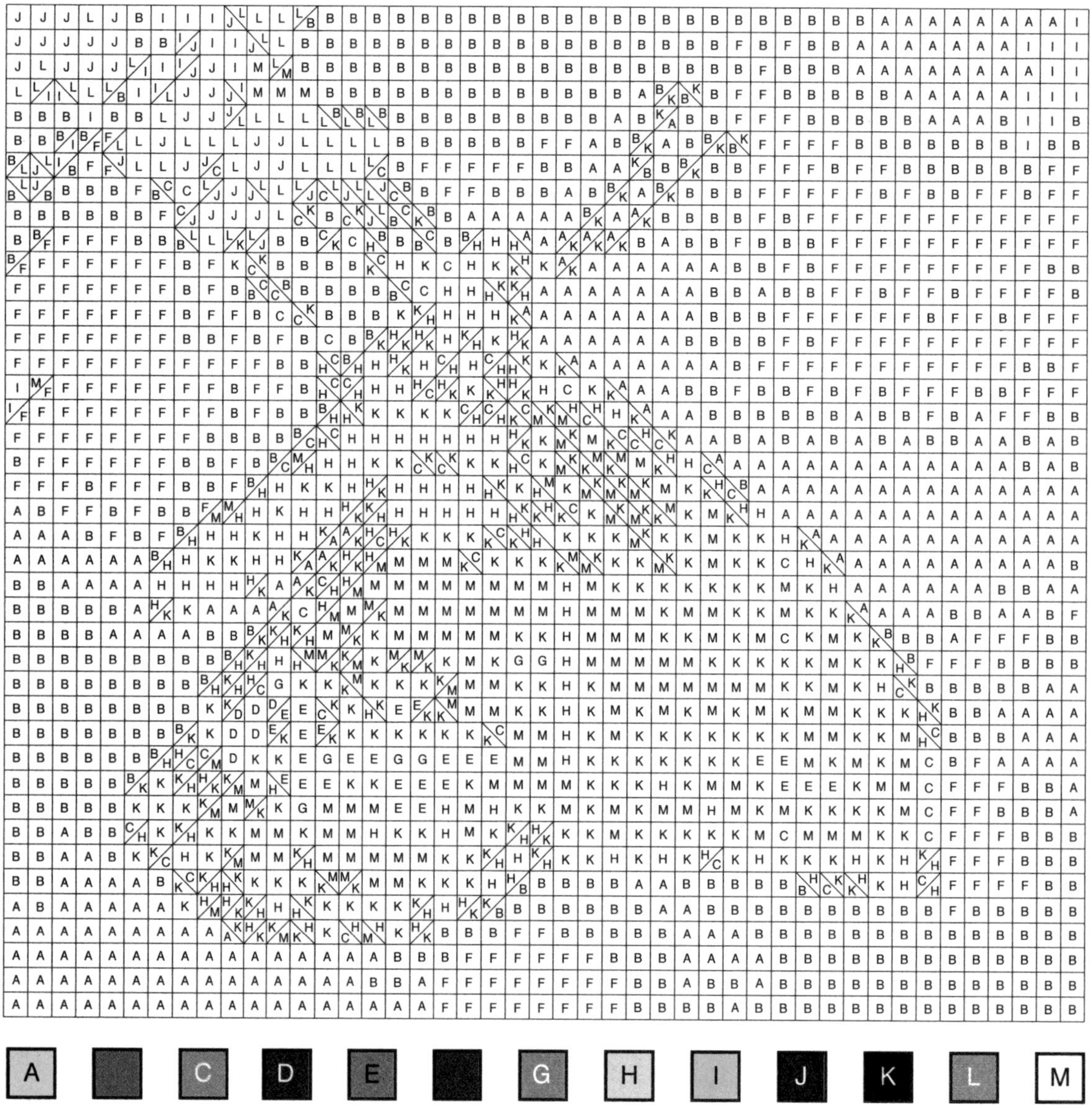

 A
 C
 D
 E
 G
 H
 I
 J
 K
 L
 M

Answer on page 119.

SWEET TART

Answer on page 119.

A LADYLIKE STROLL

EMPTY NEST SYNDROME?

Answer on page 120.

BARKING UP THE WRONG TREE

STEM THE TIDE

Answer on page 121.

LET ME CALL YOU TWEETHEART

SKY HIGH

PECKING ORDER

OUT OF YOUR GOURD

Answer on page 123.

Answer on page 124.

FINE TUNING

41

Answer on page 124.

HEADS UP!

A SHADY PRACTICE

Answer on page 125.

A PIRATE'S PAL

TRULY SUCCULENT

Answer on page 126.

Answer on page 127.

NEIGH SAYER

FRUIT OF THE VINE

ON THE SPOTS

Answer on page 128.

FROSTING OVER

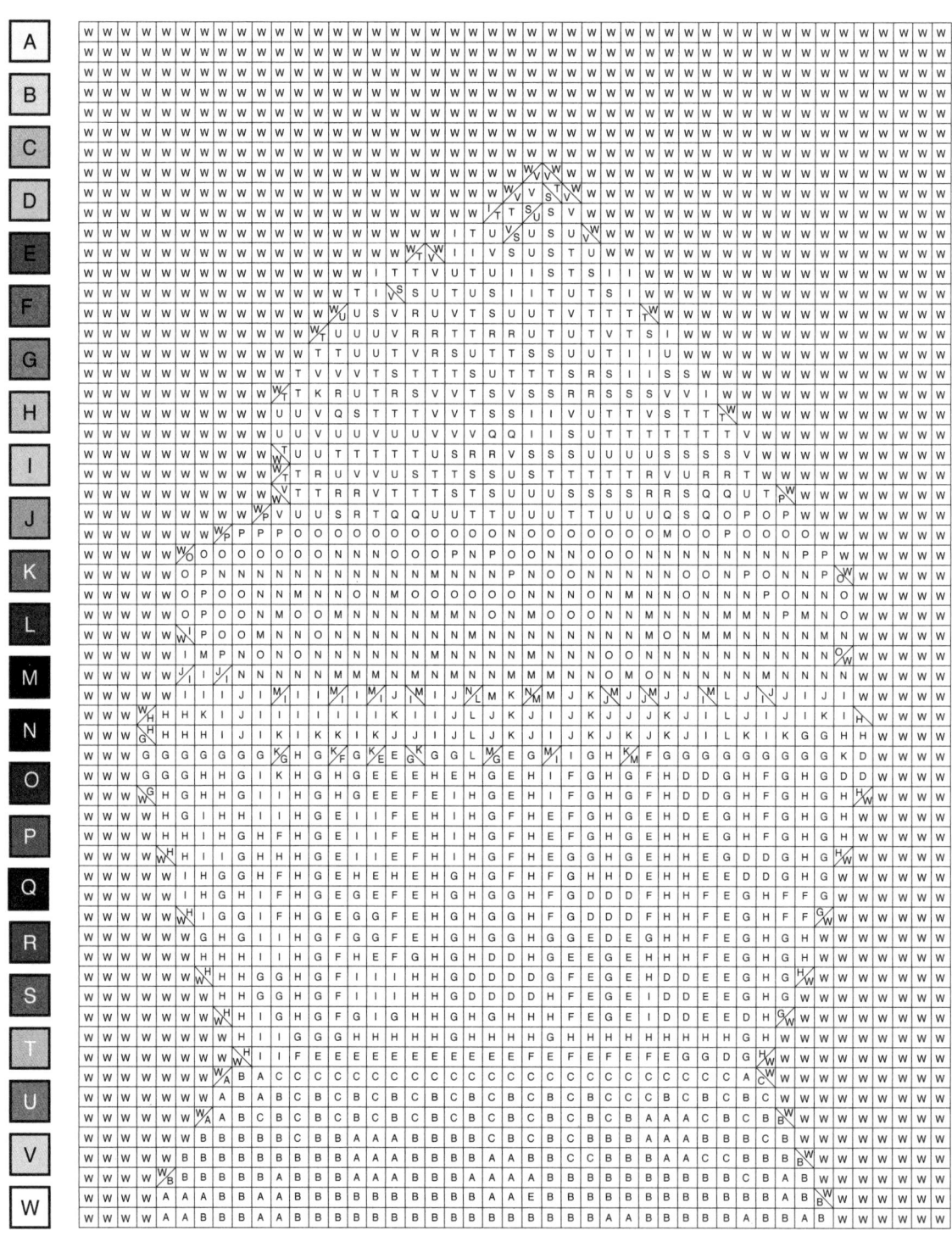

A MOOVING EXPERIENCE

Answer on page 129.

A LONG WALK...

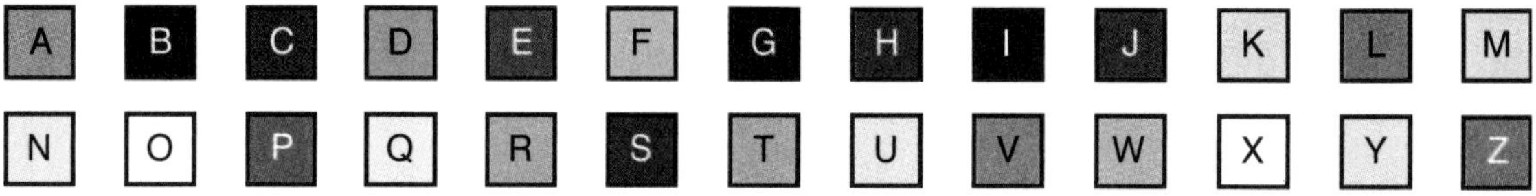

I CAN, YOU CAN, ONE CAN...

Answer on page 130.

UNPICKLED PECK

LICKETY SPLIT

Answer on page 131.

ALL RISE!

THE CARDINAL RULE

Answer on page 132.

MANICURE KIT

Answer on page 133.

PROUD PLUMES

Answer on page 133.

PETAL POWER

SILK STALKINGS

 A
 B
 C
 D
 E
 F
 J
 K
 L
 M

 N
 O
 P
 Q
 R
 S
 T
 U
V

Answer on page 134.

GETTING GRILLED

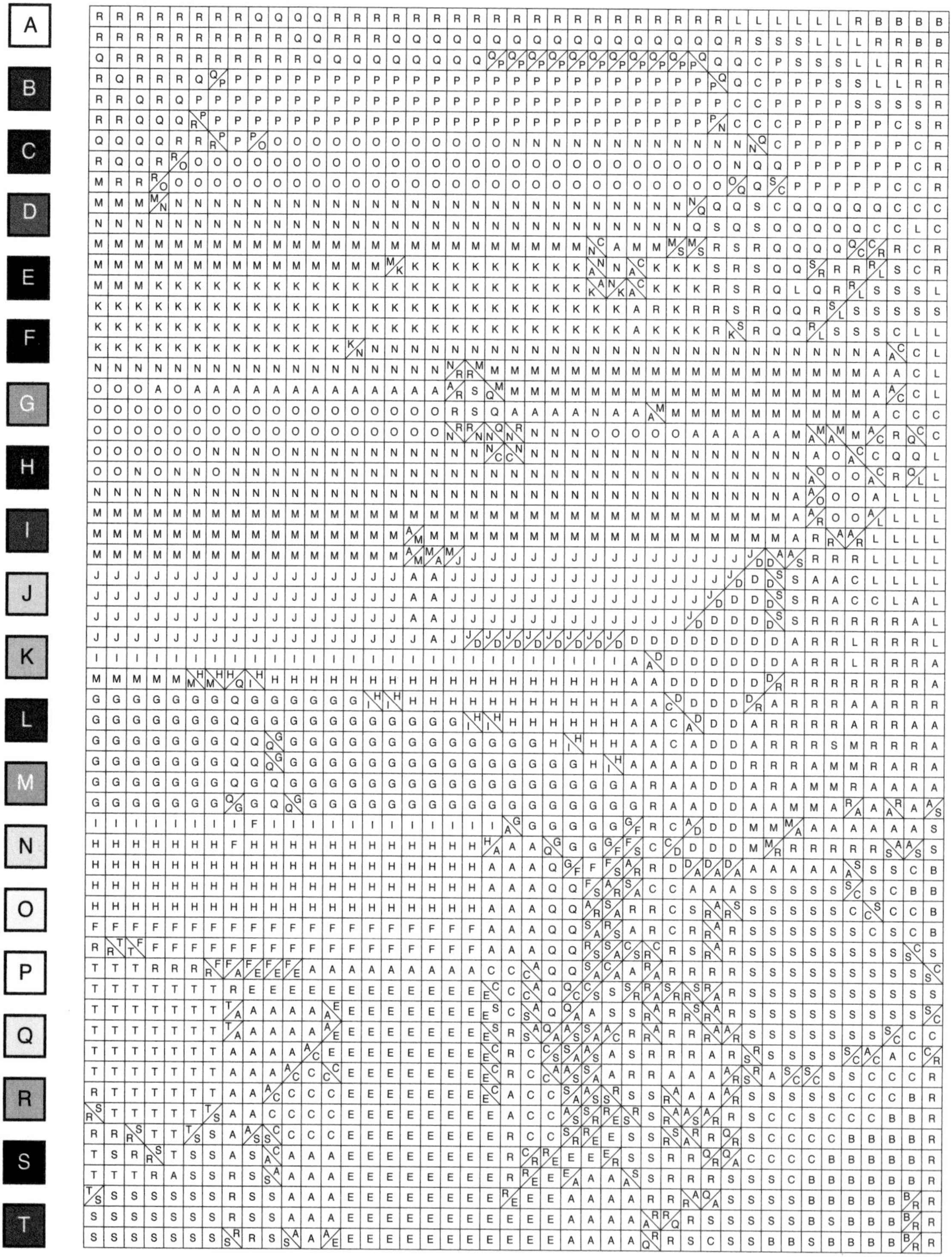

Answer on page 135.

Answer on page 135.

SMOOTH SAILING

FOWL PLAY

Answer on page 136.

KERNEL OF TRUTH

VERY FETCHING

Answer on page 137.

Answer on page 138.

COMPLETELY OVERBLOWN

RIPE FOR PICKING

Answer on page 139.

JUST KEEP SWIMMING

FLOWER FEEDER

Answer on page 140.

WORTH FRETTING OVER

Answer on page 141.

FIELD TRIP

Answer on page 142.

LUCKY LEAVES

Answer on page 143.

SLICE OF HEAVEN

81

Answer on page 144.

A TIDE-Y SUM

OPEN FOR BEES-NESS

Answer on page 145.

FIELD WORK

A
B
C
D
E
F
G
H
I
J
K
L
M
N
O
P
Q
R
S
T
U
V

C	C	C	C	C	C	C	C	C	C	C	C	C	A	C	C	C	C	C	C	C	C	C	C	C	C	C	C	C	C	C	C	C	C	C	C	C	C	C	C	C	C	C	C	C
C	C	C	C	C	C	C	C	C	C	C	C	A	C	C	C	C	A	C	C	C	C	C	C	C	C	C	C	C	C	C	C	C	C	C	C	C	C	C	C	C	C	C	C	C
C	C	C	C	C	C	C	C	A	A	A	A	A	A	A	C	A	A	A	C	C	C	C	C	C	C	C	C	C	C	C	C	C	C	C	C	C	C	C	C	C	C	C	C	C
C	C	C	C	C	A	A	A	A	A	A	A	A	A	A	A	A	A	A	C	C	C	C	C	C	C	C	C	C	C	C	C	C	C	C	C	C	C	C	C	C	C	C	C	C
C	C	C	C	C	C	A	A	A	A	A	A	A	A	A	A	A	D	D	C	C	C	C	C	C	C	C	C	C	C	C	C	C	C	C	C	C	C	C	C	C	C	C	C	C
C	C	C	C	C	A	A	A	A	A	A	A	A	A	A	A	A	A	D	C	C	C	C	C	C	C	C	C	C	C	C	C	C	C	C	C	C	C	C	C	C	C	C	C	C
C	C	C	C	C	A	A	A	A	A	A	A	A	A	A	A	A	A	D	C	C	C	C	C	C	C	C	C	C	C	C	C	C	C	C	C	C	C	C	C	C	C	C	C	C
C	C	C	C	C	C	A	A	A	A	A	A	A	A	A	A	A	A	A	D	D	C	C	C	C	C	C	C	C	C	C	C	C	C	C	C	C	C	C	C	C	C	C	C	C
C	C	C	C	C	C	C	A	A	A	A	A	A	A	A	A	A	A	A	C	C	C	C	C	C	C	C	C	C	C	C	C	C	C	C	C	C	C	C	C	C	C	C	C	C
C	C	C	A	A	A	A	A	A	A	A	A	A	A	A	A	A	A	A	A	C	C	C	C	C	C	C	C	C	C	C	C	C	C	C	C	C	C	C	C	C	C	C	C	C
B	C	C	A	A	A	A	A	A	A	A	A	A	A	A	A	A	A	A	A	C	C	C	C	C	C	C	C	C	C	C	C	C	C	C	C	C	C	C	C	C	C	C	C	C
A	B	A	A	A	A	A	A	A	A	A	A	A	A	A	A	A	C	C	C	C	C	C	C	C	C	C	C	C	C	C	C	C	C	C	C	C	C	C	C	C	C	C	C	C
A	A	B	C	A	C	A	A	A	A	A	A	A	A	C	C	C	A	B	A	C	C	C	C	C	C	C	C	C	C	C	C	C	C	C	C	C	C	C	C	C	C	C	C	C
A	A	C	C	C	A	A	A	A	A	A	A	A	A	A	B	A	B	A	B	A/D	D	D	C/D	C	C	C	C	C	C	C	C	C	C	C	C	C	C	C	C	C	C	C	C	C
B	A	B	A	B	A	B	A	B	A	B	A	B	A	B	A	B	A	A	A	E	E	E	E	B	A	C	C	C	C	C	C	C	C	C	C	C	C	C	C	C	C	C	C	C
A	B	A	B	A	B	A	B	A	B	A	B	A	B	A	A	A	A	A	A	E	E	E	E	A	B	B	A	D	C	C	C	C	C	C	C	C	C	C	C	C	C	C	C	C
A	A	A	A	A	A	A	A	A	A	A	A	A	A	A	A	A	A	A	A	E	E	E	E	A	A	A	B	B	C	C	C	C	C	C	C	C	C	C	C	C	C	C	C	C
A	A	A	A	A	A	A	A	A	A	A	A	A	A	A	A	A	A	A	A	D	D	D	D	A	A	A	A	B	C	C	C	C	C	C	C	C	C	C	C	C	C	C	C	C
A	A	A	A	A	A	A	A	A	A	A	A	A	A	A	A	A	A	A	A/E	E	E	E	E	A/E	A	A	A	A	B	C	C	C	C	C	C	C	C	C	C	C	A	C	D	D
A	A	A	A	A	A	A	A	A	A	A	A/K	A/K	A	A	A	A	A/E	E	E	E	E	E	E	E	E	A/E	A	A	B	C	C	A	C	A	A	C	A	C	C	D	A	A	D	D
B	D	B	D	B	D	B	D	B	D	B	K	K	K	K	K	G/K	E/F	E	P	P	M	M	P	E	E	E/F	B	F	B	A	A	A	A	A	A	A	A	A	D	D	A	A	A	D
G	F	G	F	G	F	G	F	G	F	B/K	K	K	K	K	K	K	G/K	F	G/F	F/G	M	M	G/F	E/F	E/F	B	F	B	F	A	A	A	A	A	A	A	A	A	A	A	A	A	A	A
F	G	F	G	F	G	F	G	F	G	K	K	K	K	K	K	K	K	K	K	K	M	M	N	F/G	G	F	G	F	B	F	G	F	G	B	F	B	F	B	F	B	F	B	F	B
L	J	L	H	L	H	L	H	L	H/K	K	K	K	K	K	K	K	K	K	K	K	M	P	N	K	K	K	B/K	G	F	G	B	G	B	F	B	F	B	F	B	F	B	F	B	F
J	L	J	L	H	L	H	L	H	K/L	K	K	K/H	K	K	K	K	K	K	K	K	N	P	N	K	K	K	K	K	K	K	K	B/K	F	B	F	B	F	B	F	B	F	B	F	B
L	J	L	J	L	J	L	H	L	H	K/L	K/H	L	K/H	K	K	K	K	K	K	K	N	P	N	K	K	K	K	K	K	K	K	K	K	J	L	J	L	H	L	H	L	H	L	H
G	L	J	L	J	L	J	L	J	L	J	L	H	J	H	K/J	K	K	K	K	K	K	K	K	K	K	K	K	K	K	K	K	K	K	L/K	J	L	J	L	H	L	H	L	H	L
I	G	I	G	I	J	L	J	L	J	L	G	J	L	J	L	K/J	K	K	K	K	K	K	K	K	K	K	K	K	K	K	K	K	K	K/J	L	J	L	J	L	J	L	J	L	H
G	I	G	I	G	I	G	I	G	I	J	I	G	J	L	J	L	K	K	K	K	K	K	K	K	K	K	K/L	H	L	H	L	H	L	J	L	J	L	J	L	J	L	J	L
J	G	J	G	J	G	I	G	I	G	I	G	I	G	J	L	I	K	K	K	K	K	K	K	K	K/J	L	J	L	H	L	H	L	H	L	H	L	H	L	J	L	J	L	J
G	J	G	J	G	J	G	J	G	J	G	I	G	I	G	I	L	K	K	K	K	K	K	K	K	L	J	L	J	L	J	L	H	L	H	L	H	L	H	L	H	L	J	L
Q	L	J	L	J	L	J	G	J	G	J	G	J	G	J	G	I	K	K	K	K	K	K	K	K	J	L	J	L	J	L	J	L	J	L	J	L	H	L	H	L	H	L	H
L	Q	L	Q	L	Q	L	Q	G	J	G	J	G	J	G	J	G	K	K	K	K	K	K	K	K	L	J	L	J	L	J	L	J	L	J	L	J	L	J	L	H	L	H	L
Q	L	Q	L	Q	L	Q	L	Q	L	Q	L	Q	L	J	G	J	K/L	K	K	K	K	K	K	K	K	G	I	G	I	J	L	J	L	J	L	J	L	J	L	J	L	J	L	J
L	I	L	I	L	I	L	I	L	I	L	I	L	I	L	J	L	K/I	K	K	K	K	K	K	K	K	I	G	I	G	I	G	I	G	I	G	I	J	H	J	H	J	H	J	H
T	J	T	J	T	J	I	L	I	L	I	L	I	L	I	L	I	L	K	K	K	K	K	K	K	K	G	J	G	I	G	I	G	I	G	I	G	I	G	H	J	H	J	H	J
J	T	J	T	J	T	J	I	L	I	L	I	L	I	L	I	L	I	K	K	K	K	K	K	K	K	J	G	J	G	J	G	J	G	I	G	I	G	I	G	I	G	I	J	H
T	J	T	J	T	J	T	J	T	L	I	L	I	L	I	L	I	L	K	K	K	K	K	K	K	K/H	I	J	I	J	I	J	I	J	I	J	G	J	G	I	G	I	G	L	G
J	T	J	T	J	T	J	T	J	T	J	T	J	T	J	I	L	P	K	P	C	C	R	R	R	I	H	I	H	I	H	I	J	I	J	I	J	G	J	G	J	G	J	G	L
T	J	Q	L	Q	J	T	J	T	J	T	J	T	J	T	J	T	P	K	P	C	C	R	R	R/I	H	I	H	I	H	I	H	I	H	I	L	I	J	I	J	I	J	G	J	G
L	Q	L	Q	L	Q	L	Q	J	T	J	T	J	T	J	T	J	T	P	P/R	R	R	R	R	H	I	H	I	H	I	H	I	H	I	L	I	L	I	L	I	L	I	J	I	J
Q	L	Q	L	Q	L	Q	L	Q	L	Q	J	T	J	T	J	T	J	P/R	R	R	R	R	R	T	J	G	H	G	H	G	H	I	L	I	L	I	L	I	L	I	L	I	J	I
S	O	L	Q	L	Q	L	Q	L	Q	L	Q	L	Q	L	Q	L	P	R	R	R	R	R	R	J	T	J	T	J	T	L	G	L	J	L	I	L	I	L	I	L	I	L	I	L
O	S	O	S	O	S	Q	O	Q	L	Q	L	Q	L	Q	L	Q	L	R	R	R	R	R	R	T	J	T	J	T	J	T	J	G	L	J	L	G	L	I	L	I	L	I	L	I
S	O	S	O	S	U	O	S	U	Q	S	Q	L	Q	L	Q	L	U	R	R	R	R	R	R	J	T	J	T	J	T	J	T	J	G	L	J	H	G	L	G	L	G	L	G	L
O	S	O	S	U	O	S	U	O	S	U	O	S	U	Q	L	Q	S	R	R	R	R	R	R/L	Q	L	T	J	T	J	T	J	T	J	T	L	J	L	J	L	G	L	G	L	G
S	O	S	U	O	S	U	O	S	U	O	S	U	S	O	Q	L	U	R	R	R	R	R	Q	L	Q	L	T	J	T	J	T	J	T	L	J	T	J	T	J	L	G	L	G	L
O	S	U	O	S	U	O	S	U	O	S	U	S	O	U	S	U	J	R/S	R	R	R	R	L	Q	L	Q	L	Q	L	Q	L	T	L	J	T	J	T	J	T	J	L	J	T	J
S	U	O	S	U	O	S	U	O	S	U	S	O	U	S	U	U	J	J	R	R	P	R/O	Q	L	Q	L	Q	L	Q	L	Q	L	T	L	J	T	J	T	J	T	J	T	J	T
U	O	S	U	O	S	U	O	S	U	S	O	U	S	U	J	S	U	J	R	R	P	O	P	J	L	Q	L	Q	L	Q	L	Q	L	Q	L	Q	L	J	T	J	T	J	T	J
O	S	U	O	S	U	O	J	U	S	O	U	S	O	S	J	U	S	J	R	R	P	S	P	U	S	V	S	V	U	V	O	V	Q	L	Q	L	Q	T	J	T	J	T	J	T
S	U	O	S	U	O	S	U	S	O	U	S	O	S	U	U	J	J	S	R/U	R	S	O	J	U	S	V	O	V	O	U	V	Q	V	Q	L	Q	L	Q	L	Q	T	J	T	J
U	O	S	U	O	S	U	J	S	U	J	J	S	O	U	S	U	J	U	S	R	J	G	G	G	O	O	S	O	U	O	U	V	Q	V	Q	L	Q	L	Q	L	Q	L	J	T
O	S	U	O	S	U	S	S	U	J	S	O	S	O	S	U	S	U	J	S	S	J	G	G	O	V	O	S	O	U	U	S	V	S	U	V	Q	L	Q	L	Q	L	Q	L	Q
S	U	O	S	U	S	O	J	S	U	O	S	J	S	O	J	U	S	U	J	S	S	O	S	J	S	V	O	U	V	U	U	S	V	S	U	V	U	V	Q	L	Q	L	Q	L
U	O	S	U	S	O	U	S	U	J	S	O	J	S	O	U	J	U	S	U	J	S	O	S	J	O	V	S	U	V	O	V	U	S	V	S	U	V	U	V	Q	V	Q	L	Q
O	S	U	S	O	U	S	J	S	U	O	S	S	O	S	J	U	J	U	S	U	J	S	U	S	V	O	S	V	U	O	U	S	U	S	V	S	U	V	U	V	S	V	S	U
S	O	S	O	U	S	U	S	U	J	S	O	S	O	S	U	J	U	J	U	S	J	S	U	S	V	O	O	V	U	V	V	U	S	V	S	V	S	U	V	U	V	S	L	V
O	S	O	U	S	U	S	J	O	U	O	S	J	S	O	J	U	S	U	J	U	S	O	S	J	O	V	S	U	V	V	U	S	U	S	U	S	V	S	U	V	S	U	S	L
Q	L	Q	L	Q	L	Q	L	Q	L	Q	L	J	S	O	U	J	U	S	U	J	S	O	S	J	O	V	S	U	V	O	V	U	S	U	S	V	S	V	S	U	V	S	V	S

Answer on page 146.

BY A NOSE

Answer on page 146.

THE ONE ON TOP

...AND SYMPATHY

Answer on page 147.

IN THE WIND

TALL AND TWIGGY

Answer on page 148.

THE SEED OF YESTERDAY

BEACH OF ETIQUETTE

Answer on page 149.

LET'S TALK TURKEY

A
B
C
D
E
G
H
I
J
K
L
M
N
O
P
Q
R
S
T
U
V
W
X
Y
Z

C	C	C	B	P	P	P	P	M	C	C	C	C	C	C	C	B	P	O	O	P	B	C	C	C	C	C	C	B	P	L	P	B/C	C	C	C	C	C	C	C	C	C	C/B	P	O
P/C	C	C/P	B	P	P	P	M	M	K/C	C	C	C	C	C	C/Q	B	P	O	O	P	B	Q/C	C	C	C	C	C/P	B	P	L	P	B	C	C	C	C	C	C	C	C	C/P	B	P	O
P	P	P	B	M	M	M	M	K	P	B	P	C	C	C/J	J	Q	P	O	O	P	Q	J	J/C	C	C	C/P	O	P	P	L	P	P	C	C	C	C	C	C	C	C/P	P	P	P	O
B	B	B	B/M	M	M	L	K	M	A	K	M	J	B	J	B	J	J	O	O	B	J	B	J	J	P	P	P	O	P	L	P	P/Q	Q	B	C	C	C/P	P	P	P	P	P	P	O
M	M	M	M	M	L	K	M	A	K	M	J	J	B	J	B	J	B	J	B	B	J	B	J	J	J	L	B	P	O	O	Q	Q	J	J	J	B	B	B	B	B	B	B	B	B
K	K	K	K	L	L	M	A	K	M	J	J	B	J	J	B	J	B	J	B	B	J	J	B	J	J	N	L	O	P	O	O	Q	Q	Q	J	J	J	B	B	B	B	B	B	B
K	K	L	L	L	K	A	K	L	I	I	I	R	I	R	I	I	R	R	R	I	R	I	R	I	I	I	N	L	O	P	O	O	O	Q	L	L	B	B	B	B	B	B	B	B
K	L	L	L	K	A	K	L	I	I	I	R	I	I	R	I	I	R	R	R	I	R	I	I	R	I	I	I	N	K	O	O	O	O	O	L	L	R	R	Q	Q	Q	Q	Q	Q
L	L	K	K	A	K	L	H	H	H	H	R	H	H	R	H	R	H	R	R	H	R	H	H	R	H	H	H	H	N	K	K	O	O	K	O	O	R	R	R	R	R	R	R	R
L	K	K	A	K	K	H	H	H	H	R	H	H	R	H	H	R	H	R	R	H	H	R	H	H	R	H	H	H	H	N	K	K	O	O	K	O	O	R	R	R	R	R	R	R
K	K	A	K	K	G	G	G	G	G	R	G	G	R	G	G	R	G	R	R	G	G	R	G	G	R	G	G	G	G	N	N	K	K	O	O	K	K	O	O	R	R	R	R	R
K	A	K	K	E	E	E	E	E	R	E	E	E	R	E	E	R	E	R	E	R	E	R	E	E	E	R	E	E	E	E	N	N	K	K	O	O	K	O	O	O	O	R	R	R
A	K	K	E	E	E	E	E	E	R	E	E	R	E	E	R	E	E	R	E	R	E	E	R	E	E	R	E	E	E	E	E	N	N	K	K	O	O	K	K	O	O	O	R	R
K	K	D	D	D	D	D	D	R	D	D	D	R	D	D	R	D	D	R	D	R	D	D	R	D	D	D	R	D	D	D	D	D	N	N	K	K	O	O	K	K	O	O	O	R
K	D	D	D	D	D	D	D	R	D	D	D	R	D	D	R	D	D	R	D	R	D	D	R	D	D	D	R	D	D	D	D	D	D	N	N	O	O	O	O	K	K	K	O	O
D	D	D	D	D	D	D	R	D	D	D	R	D	D	D	R	D	D	R	D	D	R	D	D	R	D	D	D	R	D	D	D	D	D	D	N	N	O	O	O	O	K	K	K	O
D	D	D	D	D	D	D	R	D	D	D	R	D	D	R	D	D	D	R	D	D	R	D	D	R	D	D	D	R	D	D	D	D	D	D	D	N	N	O	O	O	O	K	K	K
A	A	A	A	A	A	R	A	A	A	A	R	A	A	R	A	A	A	R	A	A	R	A	A	R	A	A	A	A	R	A	A	A	A	A	A	A	N	N	O	O	O	O	K	K
A	A	A	A	A	A	R	A	A	A	R	A	A	A	R	A	A	A	R	A	A	R	A	A	A	R	A	A	A	R	A	A	A	A	A	A	A	A	N	N	O	O	O	O	K
A	A	A	A	A	R	A	A	A	A	R	A	A	A	R	A	A	A	R	A	A	A	R	A	A	R	A	A	A	A	R	A	A	A	A	A	A	A	A	N	N	O	O	O	O
A	A	A	A	A	R	A	A	A	A	R	A	A	R	A	A	A	A	R	A	A	A	R	A	A	R	A	A	A	A	R	A	A	A	A	A	A	A	A	A	N	N	O	O	O
A	A	A	A	R	A	A	A	A	R	A	A	A	R	A	A	A	A	R	A	A	A	R	A	A	A	R	A	A	A	A	R	A	A	A	A	A	A	A	A	A	N	N	O	O
A	A	A	A	R	A	A	A	A	R	A	A	A	R	A	A	A	A	R	A	A	A	R	A	A	A	R	A	A	A	A	R	A	A	A	A	A	A	A	A	A	A	N	N	O
A	A	A	R	A	A	A	A	A	R	A	A	A	R	A	A	A	A	R	A	A	A	A	R	A	A	R	A	A	A	A	A	R	A	A	A	A	A	A	A	A	A	A	N	N
A	A	A	R	A	A	A	A	R	A	A	A	R	A	A	A	A	A	R	A	A	A	A	R	A	A	A	R	A	A	A	A	R	A	A	A	A	A	A	A	A	A	A	A	N
A	A	R	A	A	A	A	A	R	A	A	A	R	A	A/S	S	S	S/A	R	A	A	A	A	R	A	A	A	R	A	A	A	A	A	R	A	A	A	A	A	A	A	A	A	A	A
A	A	R	A	A	A	A	A	R	A	A	A	S	S	S	S	S	S	S	S	A	A	A	R	A	A	A	R	A	A	A	A	A	R	A	A	A	A	A	A	A	A	A	A	A
A	R	A	A	A	A	A	R	A	A	S	S	S	S	T	T	T	T	S	Z	Z	Z	A	A	R	A	A	A	R	A	A	A	A	A	R	A	A	A	A	A	A	A	A	A	A
A	R	A	A	A	A	A	R	A	T	S	S	T	T	T	T	T	T	T	T	T	Z	Z	Z	R	A	A	A	R	A	A	A	A	A	R	A	A	A	A	A	A	A	A	A	A
R	A	A	A	A	A	A	R	T	T	T	T	Z	Z	S	S	S	Y	Y	T	T	T	T	Z	Z	A	A	A	R	A	A	A	A	A	A	R	A	A	A	A	A	A	A	A	A
R	A	A	A	A	A	R	T	T	T	T	Z	Z	Z	Z/C	C	C/S	S	S	Y	Y	Y	T	T	Z	A	A	A	A	R	A	A	A	A	A	R	A	A	A	A	A	A	A	A	A
A	A	A	A	A	A	R	U	U	T	T	T	Z	Z	C	C	C	S	S	S	Y	Y	Y	T	T	T	A	A	A	R	A	A	A	A	A	A	R	A	A	A	A	A	A	A	A
A	A	A	A	A	R	V	V	U	U	T	T	Z	Z	Z/C	C	C/Z	S/C	C	C/S	S	Y	Y	Y	T	T	A	A	A	R	A	A	A	A	A	A	R	A	A	A	A	A	A	A	A
A	A	A	A	A	R	W	V	V	U	U	T	T	Z	Z	Z	Z	C	C	C	T	T	Y	T	T	T	A	A	A	A	R	A	A	A	A	A	A	R	A	A	A	A	A	A	A
A	A	A	A	R	W	W	W	V	V	U	U	T	T	T	T	T	T/C	C	C/T	T	T	T	U	U	U	U	A	A	A	R	A	A	A	A	A	A	R	A	A	A	A	A	A	A
A	A	A	A	R	W	W	W	V	V	V	U	U	T	T	T	T	T	T	T	U	U	U	U	U	V	V	A	A	A	R	A	A	A	A	A	A	A	R	A	A	A	A	A	A
A	A	A	A	R	X	X	W	W	V	V	V	V	U	T	T	T	T	U	U	U	U	U	V	V	V	V	A	A	A	A	R	A	A	A	A	A	A	R	A	A	A	A	A	A
A	A	A	R	A	X	X	W	W	W	V	V	V	V	U	U	U	U	U	U	U	V	V	V	V	W	X	A	A	A	A	R	A	A	A	A	A	A	A	R	A	A	A	A	A
A	A	A	R	A	X	X	X	W	W	W	V	V	V	V	V	V	V	V	V	V	V	V	W	W	X	X	A	A	A	A	R	A	A	A	A	A	A	A	R	A	A	A	A	A
A	A	A	R	A	X	X	X	X	X	W	W	W	W	W	W	W	W	W	W	W	W	W	X	X	X	X	A	A	A	A	A	R	A	A	A	A	A	A	A	R	A	A	A	A
A	A	R	A	A	A	X	X	X	X/C	C	C/W	W	W	W	W	W	W	W	W	W	X	X	X	X	X	R	A	A	A	A	A	R	A	A	A	A	A	A	A	R	A	A	A	A
A	A	R	A	A	A	X	X	X	C	C	C	W	W	W	W	W	W	W	W	X	X	X	X	X	X	R	A	A	A	A	A	R	A	A	A	A	A	A	A	A	R	A	A	A
A	A	R	A	A	A	A	X	X	X/C	C	C/X	X	X	X	X	X	X	X	X	X	X	X	X	X	A	R	A	A	A	A	A	A	R	A	A	A	A	A	A	A	R	A	A	A
A	R	A	A	A	A	A	A	X	X	X	X	X	X	X	X	X	X	X	X	X	X	X	X	A	A	R	A	A	A	A	A	A	R	A	A	A	A	A	A	A	A	R	A	A
A	R	A	A	A	A	A	A	R	X	X	X	X	X	X	X	X	X	X	X	X	X	X	A	A	A	R	A	A	A	A	A	A	R	A	A	A	A	A	A	A	A	R	A	A
A	R	A	A	A	A	A	R	A	A	C	C	C	C	C	C	C	C	C	C	C	C	A	A	A	A	A	R	A	A	A	A	A	A	R	A	A	A	A	A	A	A	A	R	A
R	A	A	A	A	A	A	R	A	A	A	C	C	C	C	C	C	C	C	C	C	A	A	A	A	A	A	R	A	A	A	A	A	A	R	A	A	A	A	A	A	A	A	R	A
R	A	A	A	A	A	A	R	A	A	A	A	A	C	C	C	C	C	C	A	A	A	A	A	A	A	A	R	A	A	A	A	A	A	R	A	A	A	A	A	A	A	A	A	R
R	A	A	A	A	A	A	R	A	A	A	A	A	A	A	A	A	R	A	A	A	A	A	A	A	A	A	R	A	A	A	A	A	A	A	R	A	A	A	A	A	A	A	A	R
A	A	A	A	A	A	R	A	A	A	A	A	A	A	A	A	A	R	A	A	A	A	A	A	A	A	A	A	R	A	A	A	A	A	A	R	A	A	A	A	A	A	A	A	A
A	A	A	A	A	A	R	A	A	A	A	A	A	A	A	A	A	R	A	A	A	A	A	A	A	A	A	A	R	A	A	A	A	A	A	R	A	A	A	A	A	A	A	A	A
A	A	A	A	A	A	R	A	A	A	A	A	A	A	A	A	A	R	A	A	A	A	A	A	A	A	A	A	R	A	A	A	A	A	A	A	R	A	A	A	A	A	A	A	A
A	A	A	A	A	A	R	A	A	A	A	A	A	A	A	A	A	R	A	A	A	A	A	A	A	A	A	A	R	A	A	A	A	A	A	A	R	A	A	A	A	A	A	A	A
A	A	A	A	A	R	A	A	A	A	A	A	A	A	A	A	A	R	A	A	A	A	A	A	A	A	A	A	A	R	A	A	A	A	A	A	R	A	A	A	A	A	A	A	A
A	A	A	A	A	R	A	A	A	A	A	A	A	A	A	A	A	R	A	A	A	A	A	A	A	A	A	A	A	R	A	A	A	A	A	A	A	R	A	A	A	A	A	A	A
A	A	A	A	A	R	A	A	A	A	A	A	A	A	A	A	A	R	A	A	A	A	A	A	A	A	A	A	A	R	A	A	A	A	A	A	A	R	A	A	A	A	A	A	A
A	A	A	A	A	R	A	A	A	A	A	A	A	A	A	A	A	R	A	A	A	A	A	A	A	A	A	A	A	R	A	A	A	A	A	A	A	R	A	A	A	A	A	A	A
A	A	A	A	R	A	A	A	A	A	A	A	A	A	A	A	A	R	A	A	A	A	A	A	A	A	A	A	A	A	R	A	A	A	A	A	A	A	R	A	A	A	A	A	A
A	A	A	A	R	A	A	A	A	A	A	A	A	A	A	A	A	R	A	A	A	A	A	A	A	A	A	A	A	A	R	A	A	A	A	A	A	A	R	A	A	A	A	A	A
A	A	A	A	R	A	A	A	A	A	A	A	A	A	A	A	A	R	A	A	A	A	A	A	A	A	A	A	A	A	R	A	A	A	A	A	A	A	R	A	A	A	A	A	A

Answer on page 150.

SPOT SHIFTER?

Answer on page 150.

GRUFF AND TUMBLE

Answer on page 151.

NEVER YOU RIND

FIT THE BILL

Answer on page 152.

A BEACON OF HOPE

SNOUT WHAT YOU THINK

Answer on page 153.

OUT FOR A SPIN

PRIME PREENING

Answer on page 154.

BURST ON THE SCENE

RIGHT IN THE KISSER

103

Answer on page 156.

FIT TO BE TIED

A B C D E F G H

SET ADRIFT

Answer on page 160.

ANSWERS

BREAKING THE ICE *(page 4)*

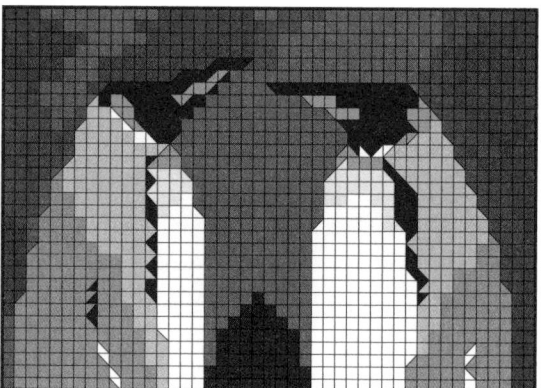

PIECE IT TOGETHER *(page 5)*

ANSWERS

A GUSTY GATHERING *(page 6)*

SUN SEEKER *(page 7)*

ANSWERS

OUT OF THE SAND *(page 8)*

WHAT GOES UP... *(page 9)*

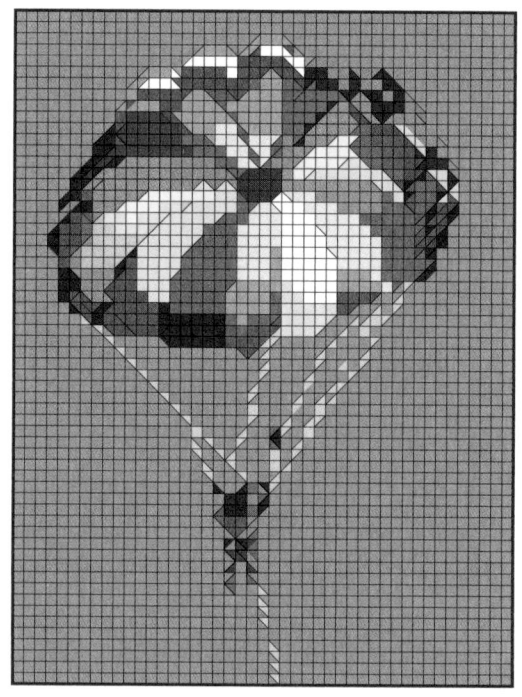

ANSWERS

LOUNGE LOVER? *(page 10)*

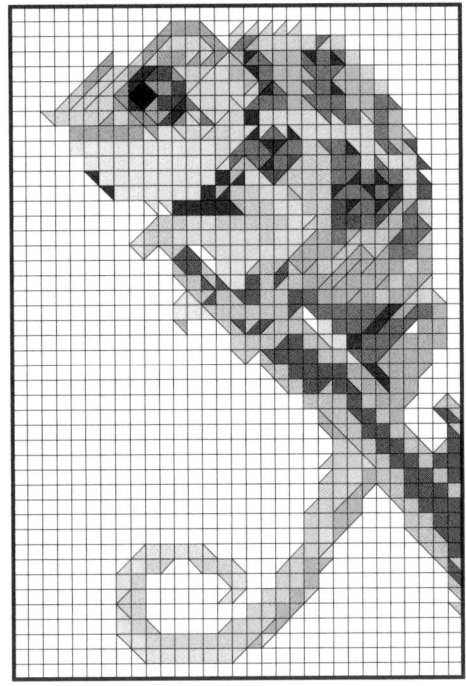

UNIVERSAL AP-PEEL *(page 11)*

ANSWERS

HOP TO IT *(page 12)*

ON THE RANGE *(page 13)*

ANSWERS

TICKLED PINK *(page 14)*

A UNIQUE ARRANGEMENT *(page 15)*

ANSWERS

ON THE PROWL *(page 16)*

WHEN IT POURS *(page 17)*

ANSWERS

OUT OF THIS WORLD *(page 18)*

 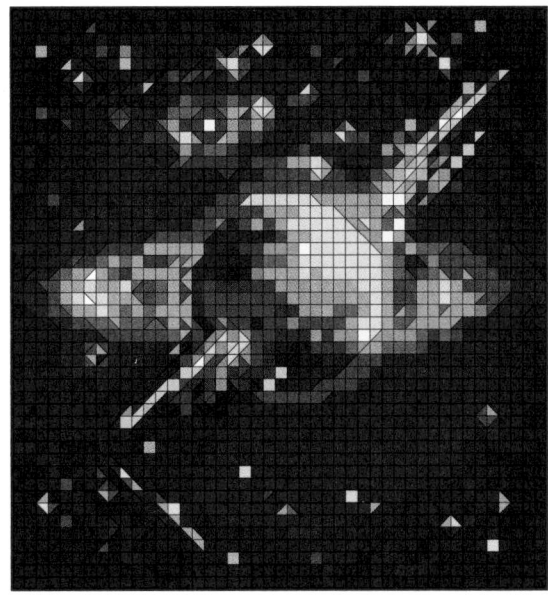

A TALL ORDER *(page 19)*

 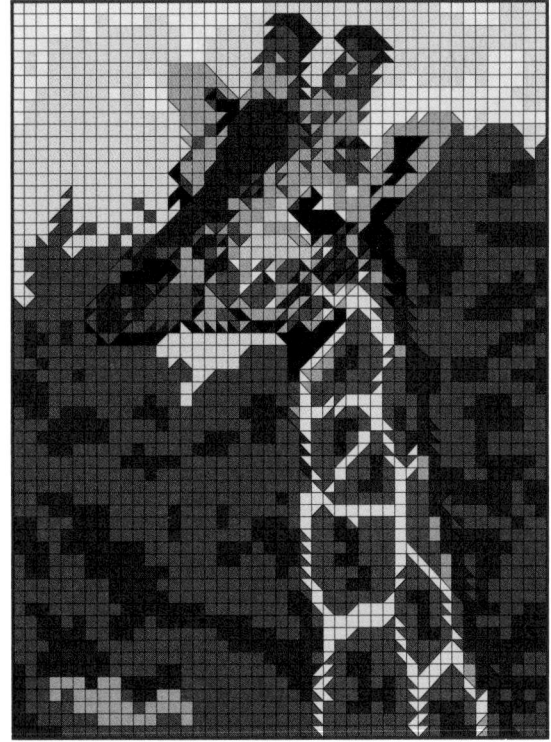

ANSWERS

ALL AFLUTTER *(page 20)*

 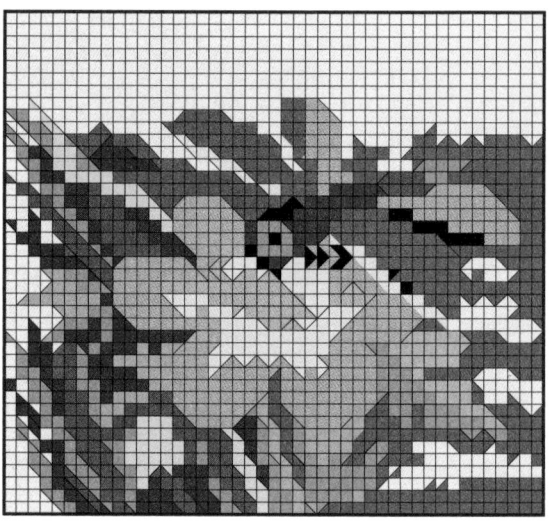

BEAM ME UP *(page 21)*

ANSWERS

MANE EVENT *(page 22)*

UP IN THE AIR *(page 23)*

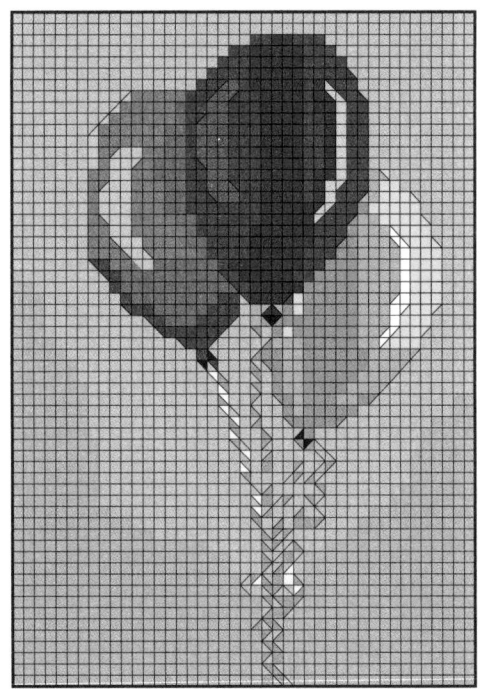

ANSWERS

TRUNK SHOW (page 24)

NEED FOR SPEED (page 25)

ANSWERS

HE LOVES ME (OR NOT) *(page 26)*

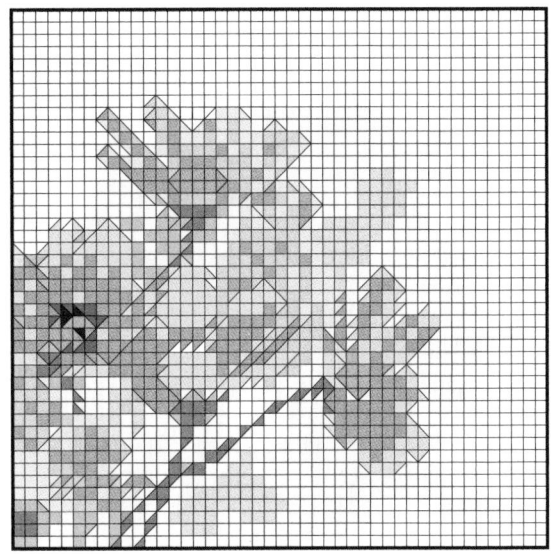

OUT OF THE BLUES *(page 27)*

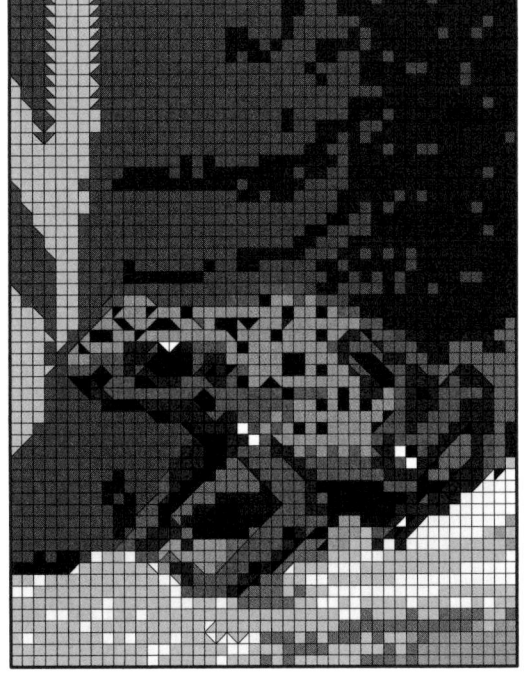

ANSWERS

TIME TO REFLECT (page 28)

ONE WAY TO GET AROUND (page 29)

 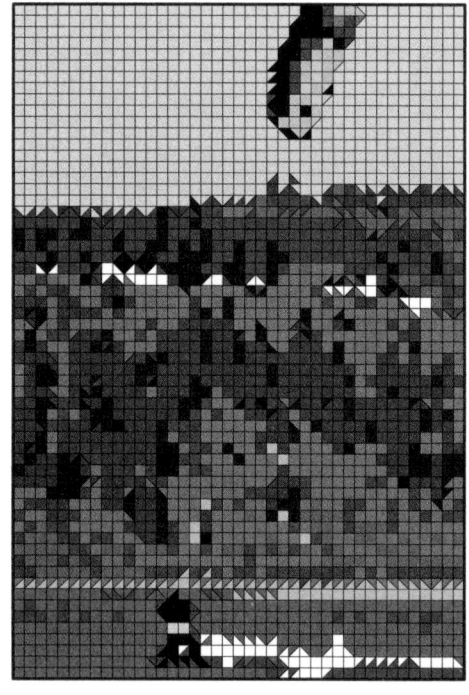

ANSWERS

NECTAR AND AMBROSIA *(page 30)*

SWEET TART *(page 31)*

ANSWERS

A LADYLIKE STROLL *(page 32)*

 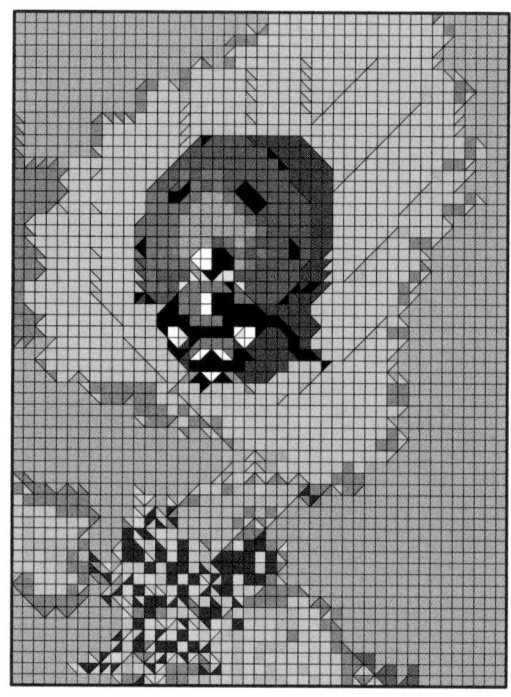

EMPTY NEST SYNDROME? *(page 33)*

ANSWERS

BARKING UP THE WRONG TREE *(page 34)*

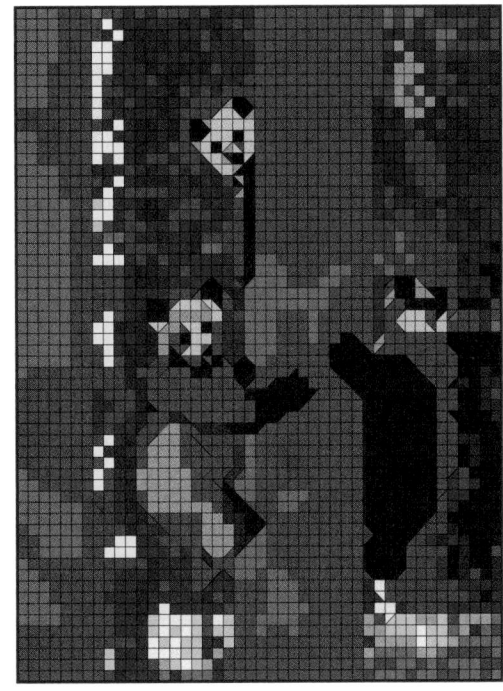

STEM THE TIDE *(page 35)*

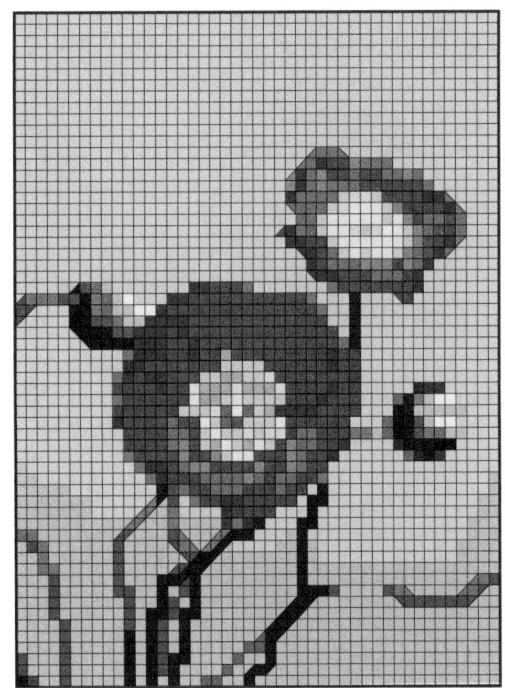

ANSWERS

LET ME CALL YOU TWEETHEART *(page 36)*

SKY HIGH *(page 37)*

ANSWERS

PECKING ORDER *(page 38)*

OUT OF YOUR GOURD *(page 39)*

ANSWERS

MONKEYING AROUND *(page 40)*

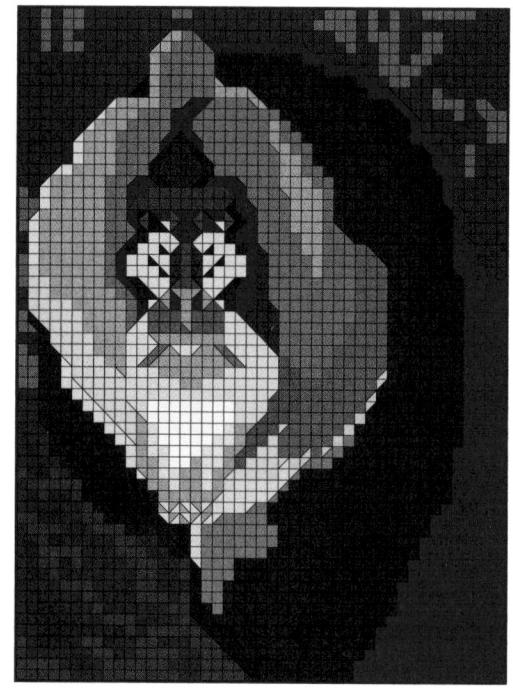

FINE TUNING *(page 41)*

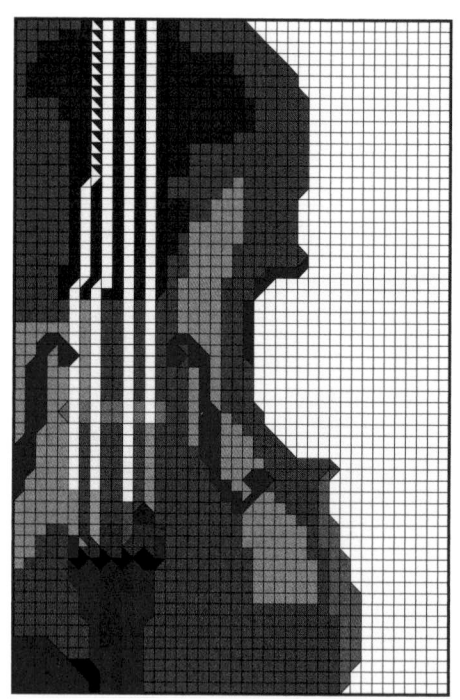

ANSWERS

HEADS UP! *(page 42)*

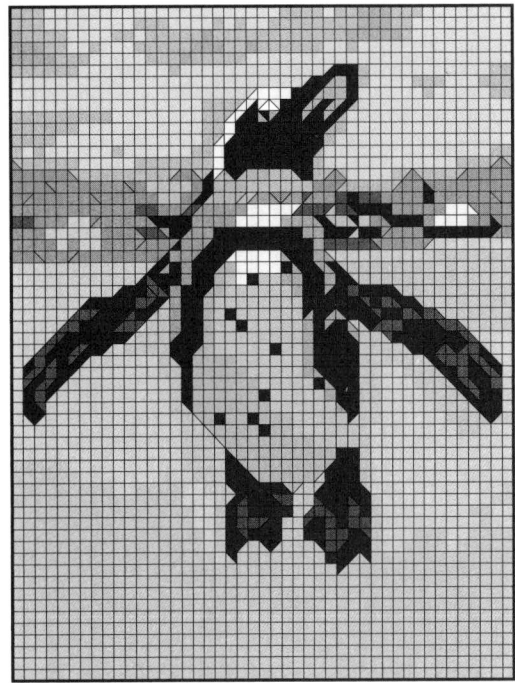

A SHADY PRACTICE *(page 43)*

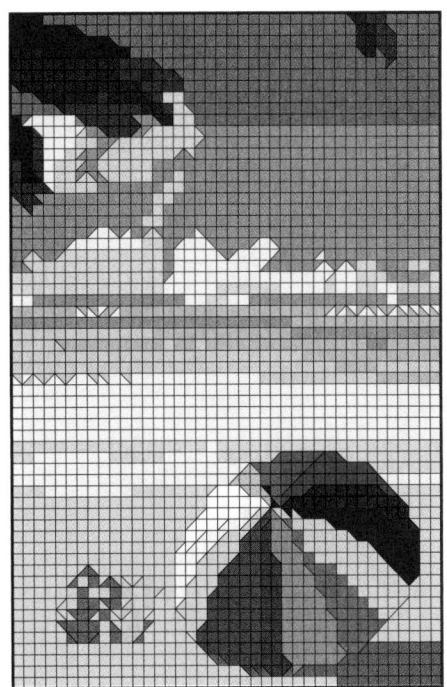

ANSWERS

A PIRATE'S PAL *(page 44)*

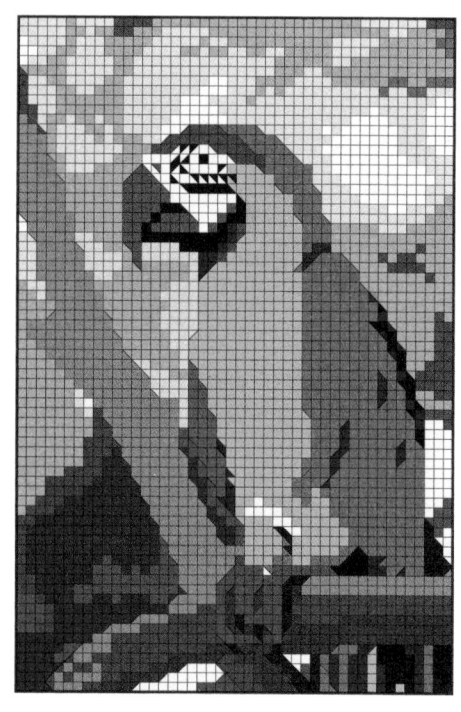

TRULY SUCCULENT *(page 45)*

ANSWERS

COURT IN SESSION *(page 46)*

 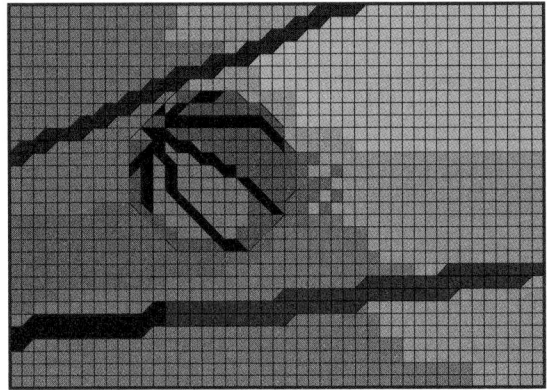

NEIGH SAYER *(page 47)*

 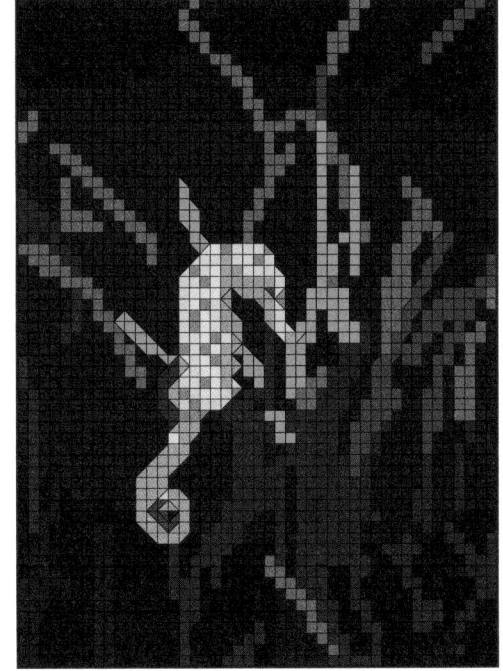

ANSWERS

FRUIT OF THE VINE *(page 48)*

 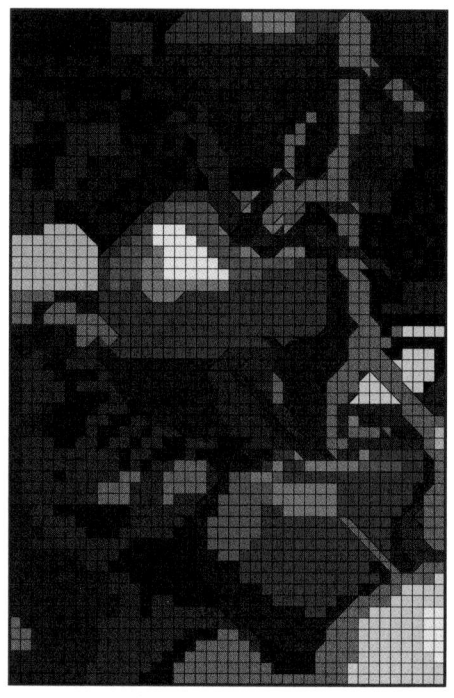

ON THE SPOTS *(page 49)*

ANSWERS

FROSTING OVER *(page 50)*

A MOOVING EXPERIENCE *(page 51)*

ANSWERS

A LONG WALK... *(page 52)*

I CAN, YOU CAN, ONE CAN... *(page 53)*

ANSWERS

UNPICKLED PECK *(page 54)*

 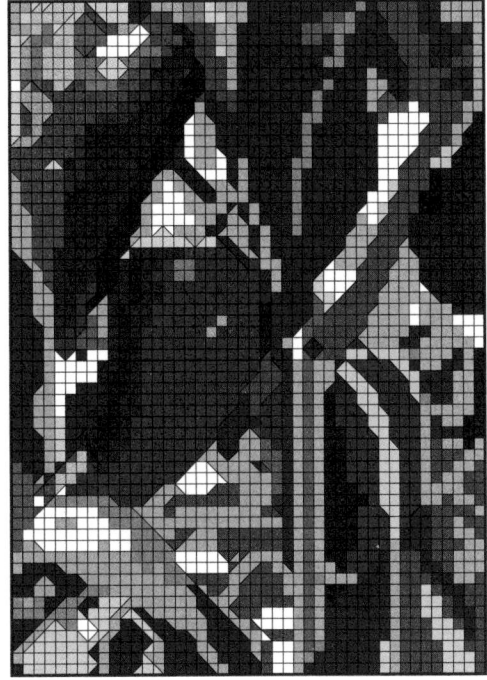

LICKETY SPLIT *(page 55)*

ANSWERS

ALL RISE! *(page 56)*

 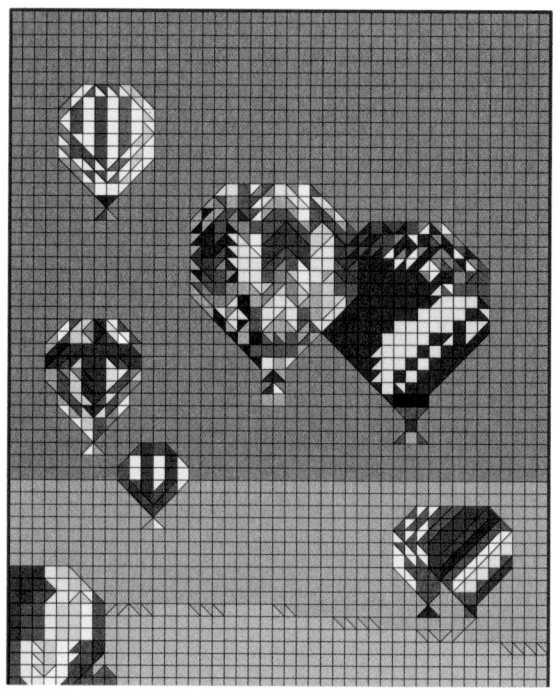

THE CARDINAL RULE *(page 57)*

 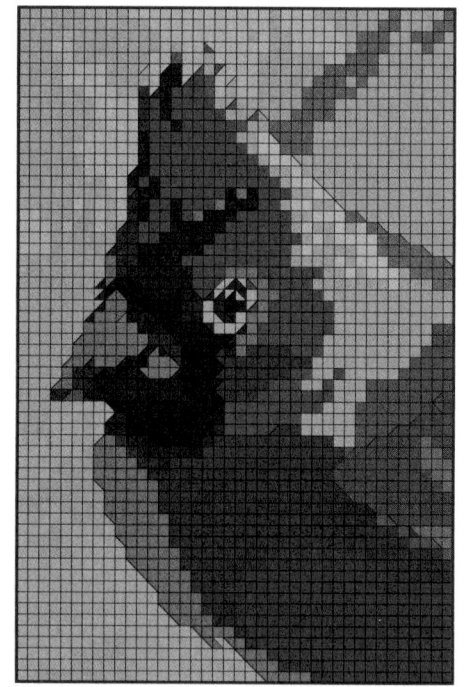

ANSWERS

MANICURE KIT *(page 58)*

 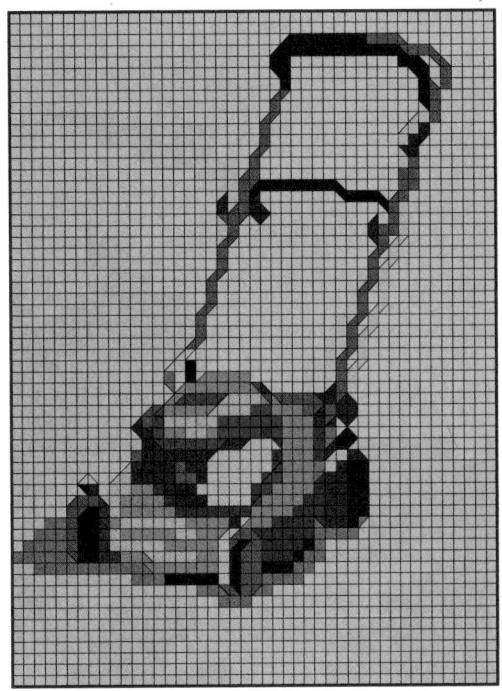

PROUD PLUMES *(page 59)*

 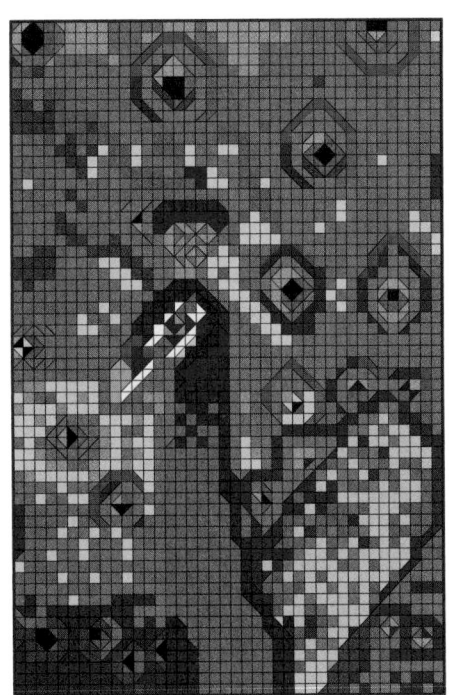

ANSWERS

PETAL POWER *(page 60)*

SILK STALKINGS *(page 61)*

ANSWERS

GETTING GRILLED *(page 62)*

AT THE DOOR *(page 63)*

ANSWERS

SMOOTH SAILING *(page 64)*

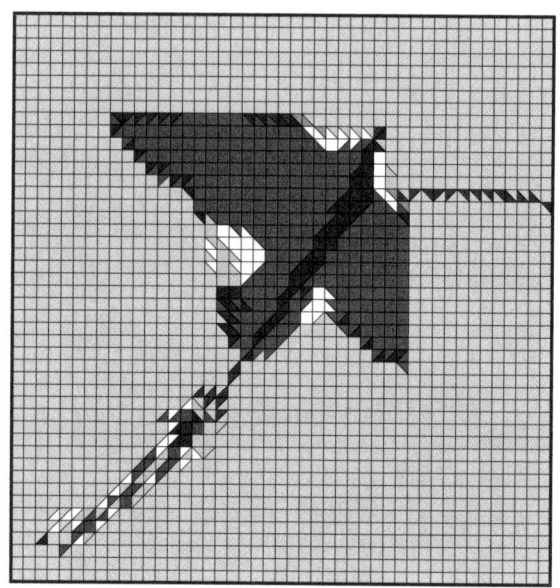

FOWL PLAY *(page 65)*

ANSWERS

KERNEL OF TRUTH *(page 66)*

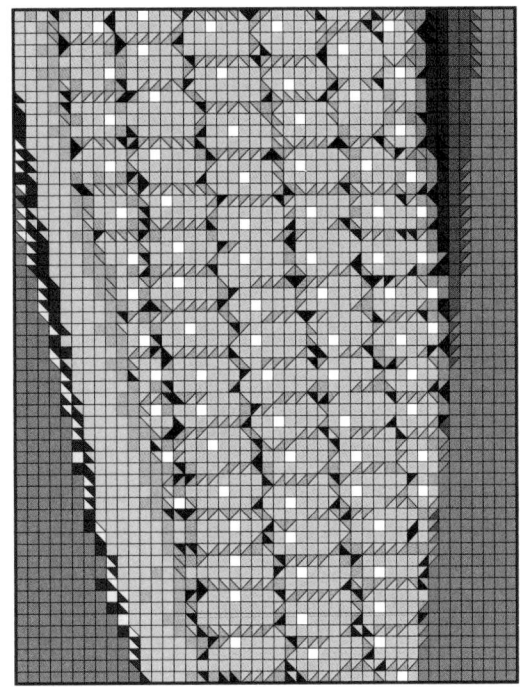

VERY FETCHING *(page 67)*

ANSWERS

PRIMARY OCCUPATION *(page 68)*

CRACKER CRAVERS *(page 69)*

ANSWERS

COMPLETELY OVERBLOWN *(page 70)*

RIPE FOR PICKING *(page 71)*

ANSWERS

JUST KEEP SWIMMING *(page 72)*

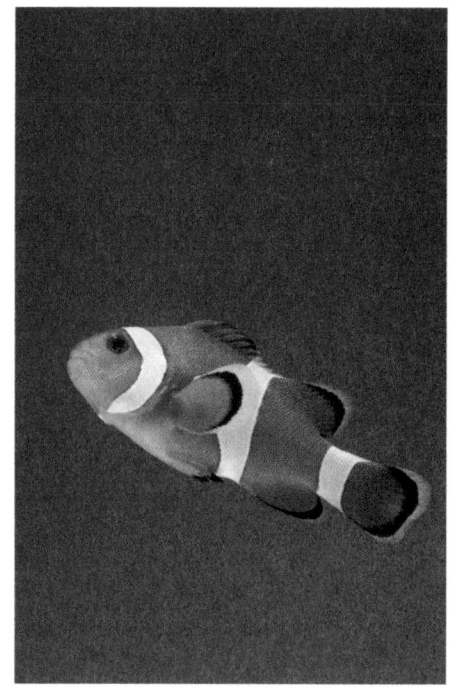 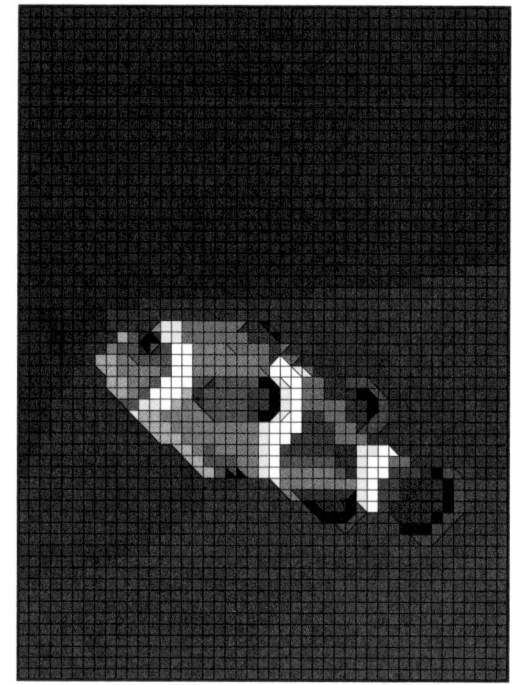

FLOWER FEEDER *(page 73)*

ANSWERS

IT'S GOT SPINE *(page 74)*

WORTH FRETTING OVER *(page 75)*

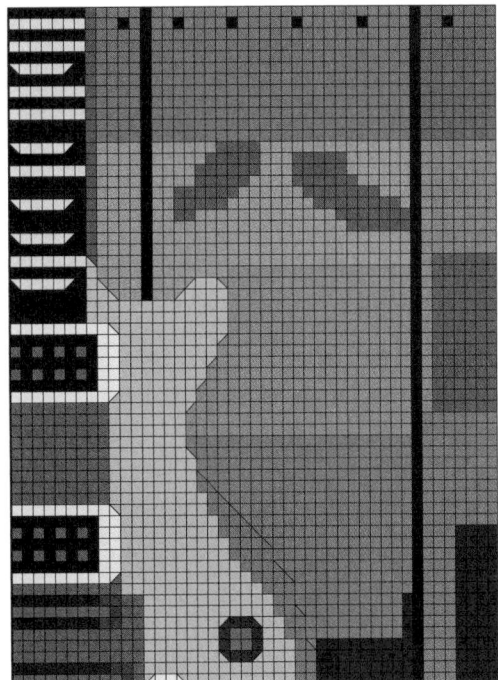

ANSWERS

FIELD TRIP *(page 76)*

IN THE JUNGLE *(page 77)*

ANSWERS

LUCKY LEAVES *(page 78)*

PRE-PRINCE PUCKER *(page 79)*

 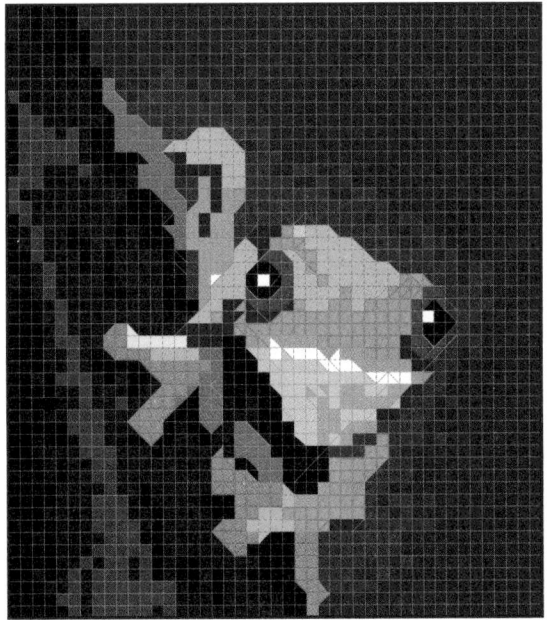

ANSWERS

SLICE OF HEAVEN *(page 80)*

 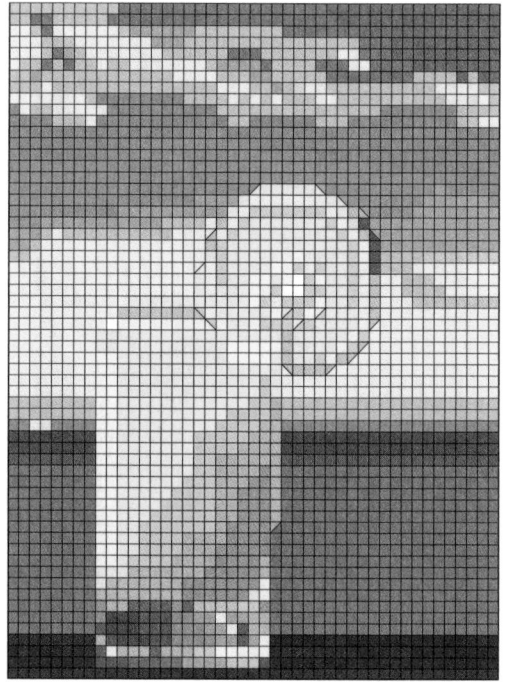

BAMBOOZLED *(page 81)*

ANSWERS

A TIDE-Y SUM *(page 82)*

OPEN FOR BEES-NESS *(page 83)*

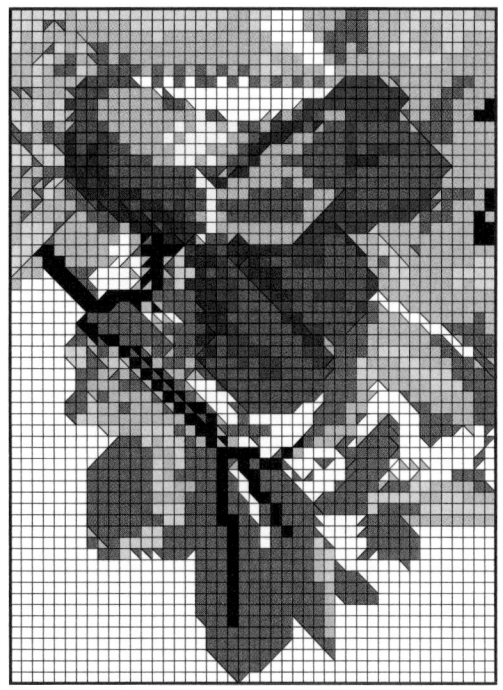

ANSWERS

FIELD WORK *(page 84)*

BY A NOSE *(page 85)*

ANSWERS

THE ONE ON TOP *(page 86)*

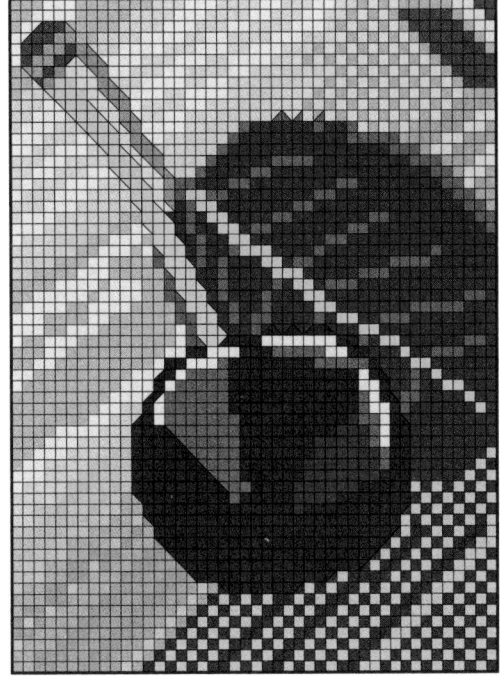

...AND SYMPATHY *(page 87)*

ANSWERS

IN THE WIND *(page 88)*

TALL AND TWIGGY *(page 89)*

ANSWERS

THE SEED OF YESTERDAY *(page 90)*

BEACH OF ETIQUETTE *(page 91)*

ANSWERS

LET'S TALK TURKEY (page 92)

 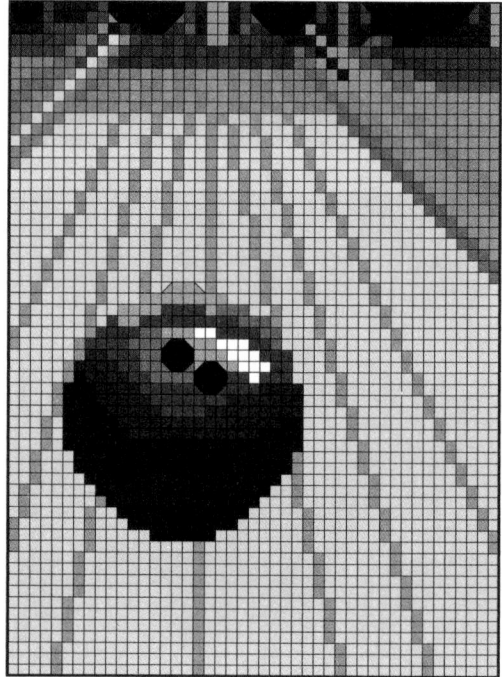

SPOT SHIFTER? (page 93)

ANSWERS

GRUFF AND TUMBLE *(page 94)*

JUST WINGING IT *(page 95)*

ANSWERS

NEVER YOU RIND *(page 96)*

FIT THE BILL *(page 97)*

ANSWERS

A BEACON OF HOPE *(page 98)*

SNOUT WHAT YOU THINK *(page 99)*

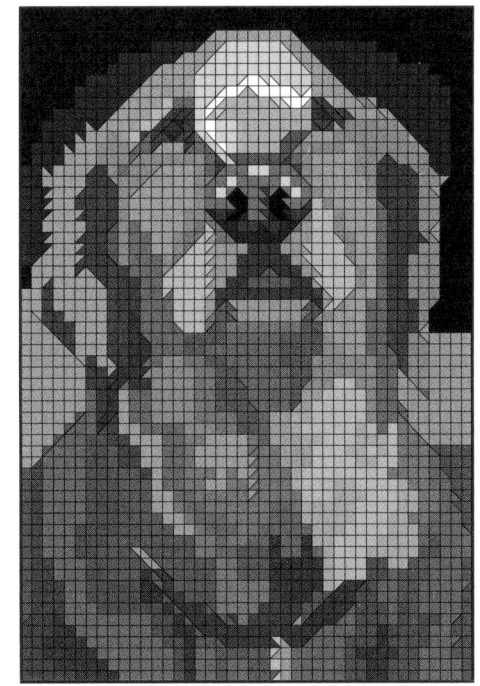

ANSWERS

OUT FOR A SPIN *(page 100)*

PRIME PREENING *(page 101)*

 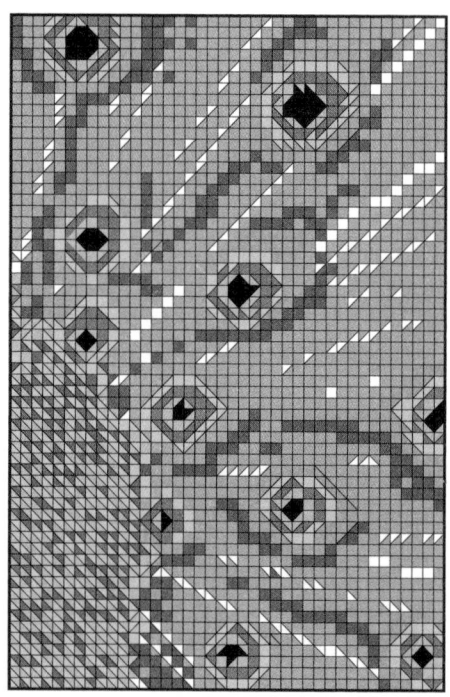

ANSWERS

BURST ON THE SCENE *(page 102)*

These swirling bubbles give the illusion of movement.

ANSWERS

RIGHT IN THE KISSER *(page 103)*

Look closely—but not too closely—at this illusion. It looks like these colors are magically bursting off the page! Move closer and farther from the image. Do you see these waves of color spin around?

ANSWERS

ANSWERS

FIT TO BE TIED *(page 104)*

Don't be fooled by this illusion. These snaky tubes may appear to be moving, but they're really stuck on the page.

ANSWERS

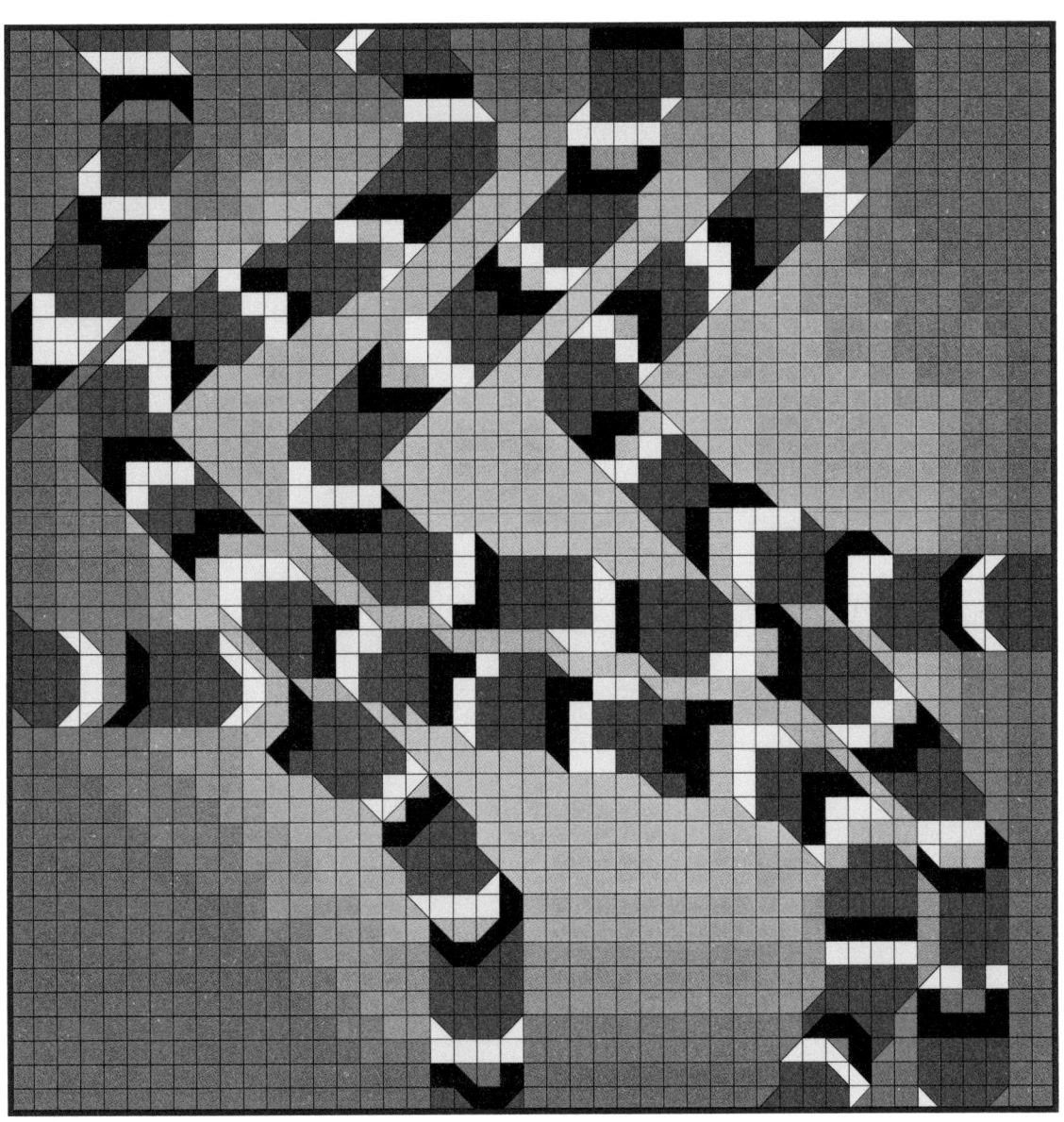

ANSWERS

SET ADRIFT *(page 105)*

Notice how the blue shapes seem to move from dark to light. Can't see any movement? Try looking at the the image with your peripheral vision as you move your head from side to side.